WOMEN IN GREEK MYTH

WOMEN IN GREEK MYTH

Mary R. Lefkowitz

The Johns Hopkins University Press
Baltimore

Johns Hopkins Paperbacks edition, 1990
2 4 6 8 9 7 5 3

The Johns Hopkins University Press
2715 North Charles Street
Baltimore, Maryland 21218-4363
www.press.jhu.edu

Library of Congress Cataloging-in-Publication Data

Lefkowitz, Mary R., 1935 –
  Women in Greek myth.

  Bibliography: p.
  Includes index.
  1. Women—Mythology.   2. Mythology, Greek.
  I. Title.
  BL795. W6L44   1986   292′.13′088042   86–7146
  ISBN 0–8018–3367–1
  ISBN 0–8018–4108–9 pbk.

Contents

DIS MANIBUS
H. L. R.

Preface

The Greeks' most important legacy is not, as we would like to think, democracy; it is their *mythology*. Even though in the first century A.D. it was announced that the god Pan was dead and mysterious voices were heard lamenting him, the Greek gods and many obscure and irrational stories about them lived on in the imaginations of artists and writers, no matter how often or in how many different ways Christians and philosophers tried to dismiss the myths as frivolous or harmful. And even in the twentieth century, when man has acquired greater power than ever before to alter the natural world, the old myths continue to haunt us, not just in the form of nymphs and shepherds on vases or garden statuary, but in many common assumptions about the shape of human experience. The notions – now presumably obsolete – that a man should be active and aggressive, a woman passive and subject to the control of the men in her family, are expressed in virtually every Greek myth, even the ones in which the women seek to gain control of their own lives. That the most important phase of a woman's life is the period immediately preceding her marriage (or re-marriage) is preserved in the plot of many novels; also the notion that virginity, or at least celibacy, offers women a kind of freedom that they are no longer entitled to when they become involved with a man.

In this book I wish not only to describe how the Greeks portrayed female experience in myth, but also to suggest why in the hands of the great poets the narrative patterns were not as restrictive as I have made them sound. I believe that it is possible to show that the Greeks at least attributed to women a capacity for understanding that we do not always find in the other great mythological tradition that has influenced us, namely, the Old and New Testaments.

There are two main reasons why we give the Greeks too little credit for their relatively balanced view of women's abilities. The first is that most of us encounter Greek mythology only in a condensed and filtered form, at best in a translation of some work of literature, but more often as stories retold in a modern handbook. Inevitably, in the process of condensation and translation, the original meaning can easily get lost. For example, it is very hard to know what can be deduced from the story of the prophet Tiresias' famous statement that women get more pleasure out of the sexual act than men. The story was first told in an epic poem of the sixth century B.C., now lost, the Hesiodic *Melampodia*; only two lines of it survive: 'Of ten shares the man enjoys one, the woman by enjoying ten satisfies her mind (*noêma*)' (fr.275MW). According to the outline of the original version that writers of the third century B.C. give us, Tiresias, who had been both a man and a woman, was asked by Zeus to say whether women or men got more pleasure out of intercourse, and because of his answer Hera blinded him and Zeus then, in compensation, gave him the power of prophecy. How are we to interpret this story? Did Hera blind him because he revealed some mystery? Does the story imply that because women were said to have enjoyed intercourse more they were more eager for it, and had to be watched more carefully? Or is it, as comparative anthropology would suggest, intended as an explanation of why bards often behaved and dressed in a female manner, and indeed had to understand both male and female experience in order to be able to prophesy accurately? Transvestism in ritual often marks a critical change, as from puberty to adulthood; it can also, as in the case of Pentheus in the *Bacchae*, mark one for destruction; in either case it helps the one who changes to acquire a privileged, otherwise inaccessible knowledge (Burkert 1979, 30). Thus while it is possible to say that the story of Tiresias puts female sexuality in a bad light, it may also be possible to say that the story affirms that there were rewards and reasons to acquire female identity.

The second, and more insidious, reason why myth tends to be misunderstood derives from the concerns and beliefs of our own society. Even when myths about women are preserved in surviving works of ancient literature, so that we can have some idea of how the authors at least meant them to be understood, our own assumptions about what myth ought to mean can lead us to place undue emphasis on factors the ancients themselves were not aware of. Psychologists tend to assume that human nature has for all time remained basically the same, and therefore conclude that the ancients were preoccupied with much the same problems as we are, namely, sex, and the definition and role of the sexes. But it is another question whether the ancients themselves would have understood or accepted interpretations that place primary emphasis on the role of desire and incest. The text of Sophocles' *Oedipus Tyrannus* gives no indication that Oedipus was sexually attracted to Jocasta; he married her because marriage to the king's widow was the reward for ridding Thebes of the Sphinx. Similarly, I think, Thyestes has intercourse with his daughter not because he is in love with her, but because the Delphic oracle told him that the son born from this union would take revenge on Thyestes' brother Atreus, for murdering Thyestes' other children. The son, Aegisthus, seduces Clytemnestra and murders Atreus' son Agamemnon, and so gets back his own father's kingdom; in each generation inheritance and power are more compelling motives than sex.

Feminists tend to reject the psychologists' premise that man's preoccupations have not changed over time, and prefer instead to discover in the myths evidence of the persistent limitations of human imagination, in particular a tendency to think in polar opposites that can, by association, organise experience into certain restricted channels, much as a language might forbid some particular grammatical usages in favour of others that are inherently no more worthy than those it has excluded. But I do not believe that Sophocles would have been aware – as has recently been claimed – that in the *Oedipus Tyrannus* he was primarily concerned with incest, or an excessive endogamy that ends in sterility and the extinction of his family (duBois 1981, 103; Goldhill 1984, 197). It is true that in this myth incest leads to destruction. Oedipus' sons by his mother Jocasta, Eteocles and Polynices, kill each other in single combat; his daughter Antigone dies because she seeks, against her uncle Creon's orders, to bury her brother Polynices' body. But in the *Antigone* Sophocles speaks only about the inexorable progress of the family curse, from which no generation can free itself, which he calls 'folly in speech and a fury in the mind'. Other critics, looking at the same myth and concentrating on references in it to lameness and maiming, have suggested instead that the story of

Oedipus' family concerned the question of the origin of man: was he born from woman, or from the earth, like plants? (Lévi-Strauss 1955, 91-2; Segal 1982, 180-5).

But where modern critics would emphasise either sexual or social issues, the poet himself speaks of *perceptual* and *ethical* problems: will man know what is right, and even if he does, will he do it? Sophocles' answer is unequivocally negative:

Hope in its many wanderings is a help to some men, but to others it is the deception that comes from vain passions. It comes on a man who knows nothing until he burns his foot in the hot fire. In wisdom once – from some unknown person – a famous statement came to light: 'evil seems good to the person whose wits the god is leading towards delusion (*atê*); he acts only for the shortest time apart from delusion.' (615-25)

The chorus does not say specifically that these lines apply to any particular character in the play, but since they are talking about the house of Oedipus it is natural to assume that they have Antigone in mind, though it soon turns out that their words apply equally well to Creon, the king who has condemned her to death for trying to bury her brother against his orders; his decision will cause the death of *his* family as well. The point is that – at least so far as the Greeks themselves were concerned – the human condition – not gender – causes the problems that men and women both are bound to experience, especially if they try to accomplish something out of the ordinary.

In this book I want to suggest that it may not be profitable to regard the myths as a kind of code that could be reliably deciphered were we to apply the right modern methodology. Whatever the story of Oedipus may have meant when it was first told, whenever that was, by the time the poems of Homer were composed, it and virtually every other myth were presumed to belong to a distant past. The myths had become a kind of history, and they were retold both for entertainment and for instruction, often with conclusion first (since everyone knew how the story would end): even an extraordinarily long narrative, like the *Odyssey*, begins by stating that Odysseus returned home after wandering and learning much, but having lost his companions because of their own folly. Modern critics may discern in Odysseus' adventures a covert description of the development of the human psyche, but the Greeks themselves

understood it first as a moral tale, where the evil suitors were
defeated by the courage and intelligence not only of Odysseus,
but also of his wife Penelope, to whom – in spite of an offer of
immortality from the goddess Calypso – he was eager to return.
Before I begin, I should make explicit two aspects of my
approach to myth. (1) It must be stressed that the Greeks, unlike
certain story-tellers in cultures without developed literary
traditions, are admirably able to speak for themselves, and that
we are therefore not easily justified in assuming that they meant
something other than, or beyond, what they actually said. For
that reason, in the discussion that follows, I am not going to try
to interpret myths that survive only in summary or quotation,
where we cannot know or recover the emphasis in the original. (2)
I shall also try to distinguish, whenever possible, between literal
and mythical meaning. We should not immediately assume that
everyday action is described in myth, and that normal relations
between the sexes are always represented. When these stories are
told in epic or in drama, they are set either in a remote past or a
remote place; the characters are not ordinary people, but heroes.
When these stories are enacted in ritual, clear lines of
demarcation are observed. In certain myths connected with
Dionysus, such as the story of king Lycurgus in *Iliad* 6, a man
pursues a group of women with intent to harm them, but they
escape (130-40). But in the festival of Agrionia in Boeotia, when
the priest Zoilus, carried away by excitement during the
performance of the ritual, killed one of the maidens he was
pursuing, he fell ill and died, and the town was beset by lawsuits;
so the priesthood was taken away from his family (Plutarch,
Moralia 299e-300a=*WLGR* 244). For reasons that are not
explained here or in other accounts of myth and rituals involving
Dionysus, it is the pursuit that matters, and bloodshed, while
threatened, is better avoided (Burkert 1983, 173-7). In the myths
that involve the pursuit of women by a man the women are
described as 'maddened' and have left their normal pursuits of
weaving and child care to wander in the wilderness. The male
pursues them and threatens to punish them, and in cases where
he does not manage to kill the women (or the women kill him or
someone else), the women contrive to return to their homes. The
pattern of pursuit in myth does not necessarily imply the
existence of an abiding hostility between the sexes (cf. Slater
1968, 283-4; Simon 1978, 250; Segal 1982, 189-204); by contrast, it

may only suggest that the Greeks knew how to describe basic human sexual instincts, both male aggression and female submission, and believed that these must be recognised but also controlled if human beings of both sexes are to live together in harmony and understanding.

I have not tried in this book to give a comprehensive account of what happened to all women in Greek myth, or to describe every aspect of women's life that the myths describe; instead I have concentrated only on those aspects of women's experience which have been most frequently misunderstood in recent literature. I begin with the notions of matriarchy and the Amazons, then turn to women's life when they are away from men, marriage, women's role in politics, the degree of repression expressed in women's martyrdom, and finally, the nature of Greek misogyny. If my account of women's experience in myth and men's attitude towards women seems less negative than other recent work by women scholars about the ancient world, it is not because I wish to be an apologist for the past, which I am delighted not to be living in myself, but because I am trying not to read into it the standards and preoccupations of the twentieth century.

Acknowledgments for permission to reprint are due as follows. Chapter 1: *Times Literary Supplement* (Nov. 27 1981) 1399-1401. Chapter 2: *The American Scholar* (Spring 1985) 207-219. Chapter 4: *Greece & Rome* 30 (1983) 31-47. Chapter 5: *Images of Women in Antiquity*, ed. A. Cameron and A. Kuhrt (London 1983) 49-64. Chapters 3, 6, and 7 are hitherto unpublished, and the other chapters have been revised and brought up to date.

My father, who always read everything I wrote, urged me to write a book about women and myth accessible to non-specialist readers; I wish that I had been able to complete it in time for him to see it.

1985   M.R.L.

1

Princess Ida and the Amazons

No Greek myths about women have claimed so much attention in recent times as those that concern matriarchy. These myths became a subject of interest in the mid-nineteenth century, when the question of women's education began seriously to be debated. Tennyson's poem 'The Princess' (1847-51) describes the creation and demise of a woman's college; the story was parodied by Gilbert and Sullivan in the comic operetta *Princess Ida* a generation after Tennyson's poem was published. In the original 'Princess', Tennyson described a 'university for maidens', modelled along the lines of an Oxbridge college, but run entirely for and by women – a vision that was to become a reality in 1869 with the founding of what was to become Girton College. In the poem, only the founder of the college, Princess Ida, is strong enough to abide by the rules of celibacy and withdrawal that she has set, and in the end even she is called back to a woman's normal role as wife and mother, not by brute male force but by what Tennyson saw as a natural dependency on men and an instinctive female desire to nurture. Tennyson portrays the Princess's vision with great sympathy and complexity. Feminist writers today have returned to the poem because the founders of the great women's colleges both in America and England knew it, and because Tennyson describes with such clarity the principal problems of feminism not only in his own time, but in ours as well (Wells 1978, 1-5; Auerbach 1978, 4-7).

The Princess seeks first to have an environment that expresses the ideals of her institution. The statues in the great hall of her Women's College are

15

... – not of those that men desire,
Sleek Odalisques nor oracles of mode,
Nor stunted squaws of West or East, but she
That taught the Sabine how to rule, and she
The foundress of the Babylonian wall,
The Carian Artemisia strong in war,
The Rhodope that built the pyramid,
Clelia, Cornelia, with the Palmyrene
That fought Aurelian, and the Roman brows
Of Agrippina. Dwell with these, and lose
Convention, since to look on noble Forms
Makes noble thro' the sensuous organism
That which is higher. O lift your natures up;
Embrace our aims; work out your freedom. (ii.62-75)

To judge by the Library of Wellesley College, a university for women founded in 1875, the Princess's choice of statuary is most unconventional. In 1913, doors were chosen for the library with figures representing Wisdom (*Sapientia*), rather oddly, a bearded old *man* with a book, and Charity (*Caritas*), represented by a woman comforting a naked child. These doors were (and still are) flanked by matronly statues of Athena and Hestia, 'so that the goddess of wisdom was balanced by the goddess of the hearth' (Glasscock 1975, 313). The Princess, by contrast, picked women of accomplishment – rulers, builders, a general like Artemisia (Herodotus 8. 87-8) or the intrepid Cloelia who swam the Tiber (Livy 2.13.6-9), Cornelia, who educated her sons the Gracchi (Plutarch, *Tiberius Gracchus* 1.2-2), and the elder Agrippina, who stood up to the emperor Tiberius (Tacitus, *Annals* 4.35). But the Princess's speech describing them shows a certain obliviousness: Rhodope that built the pyramid made her fortune as a courtesan, if indeed she built the pyramid, which Herodotus denies (2.134).

Tennyson's narrator, Prince Hilarion in female disguise, does not comment on such inconsistencies; he is much more impressed by the beauty of the students than by the statues. But he manages to summarise a lecture that might serve as a syllabus for a present-day popular survey of Women's History. The lesson begins with a Darwinian account of human evolution (omitting God and Adam), starting with the cave man 'crushing down his mate'. Then the lecturer, Lady Psyche

Glanced at the legendary Amazon
As emblematic of a nobler age;
Appraised the Lycian custom, spoke of those
That lay at wine with Lar and Lucumo (ii.110-13)

before briefly characterising and criticising more recent civilisations, and finally prophesying a future in which men and women would work together. As in the case of the statues, the most positive models are drawn from the Greco-Roman past: the Amazons who ruled themselves and fought wars like men; the Lycians, who were said to be known by their mother's rather than their father's name, and whose citizenship is determined by their mother's status (Herodotus 1.173); and finally Cloelia (again), the girl who swam the Tiber and was praised even by her enemy Lars Porsenna, and Tanaquil, the domineering wife of Rome's fifth king, the Etruscan Lucumo or Tarquinius.

Of these legendary and mythical role models, only the Amazons have been taken seriously by feminist scholars, probably because they represent a whole society, and not just the singular achievement of an extraordinary individual. For example, Phyllis Chesler has suggested in her best-selling book *Women and Madness* that 'Amazon society was probably better for the development of women's bodies and emotions than any male-dominated society has ever been' (Chesler 1972, 286). The source for this information appears to have been a single book, Helen Diner's *Mothers and Amazons: the first feminine history of culture*, a work first circulated in English in the thirties under the pseudonym of Sir Galahad. Diner claims (1965, xiv-xv) that she consulted the ancient sources, but the way she refers to ancient historians shows that she has no notion of when they lived or whether their works still survive. Her reconstruction of Amazon society appears to have been inspired primarily by the Swiss jurist Johann Jacob Bachofen's influential treatise, *Mother Right: an investigation of the religious and juridical character of matriarchy in the ancient world*, first published in 1861. Bachofen argued that women had been the first governors of ancient societies, on the basis of the scattered references in the ancient sources to Amazons and to matrilinear societies (in which descent and property rights follow the female line).

At first sight there appears to be some evidence for Bachofen's theory: Herodotus in the fifth century B.C. speaks of an Amazon society, the Sauromatae, in Scythia, where women hunt on horseback alongside men, often wear men's clothing, and even fight in wars (4.116); a woman in this society is not allowed to marry until she has killed a man in battle (4.117). The Greek medical treatise in the Hippocratic corpus *Airs, Waters, Places*, which may be as early as the late fifth century B.C., offers a slightly different description of the Amazon tribe Sauromatae. Women ride to hunt and fight in battles so long as they are virgins, but rarely after their marriage; they must kill *three* men before they can marry. They have no right breast; these are removed by their mothers when they are babies, by cauterisation with a special bronze instrument, so that all the strength and bulk of the removed breast are directed to the right shoulder and arm (ch. xvii, *CMG* I 12). In the treatise *Articulations* (on the joints of the body), we are told that some authorities relate that the Amazons disjoint the lower extremities of male infants in order to render them lame (53, L IV 232). A commentary on Homer that has its origins in the third century B.C. adds that the Amazons fed their babies with tortoises, lizards and snakes, since they did not use breasts (schol. *Il* 3.189). Diner (1965, 127-8) was able to deduce from this kind of information that Amazons not only did not nurse their children but did not raise them, and that retaining the left breast was an affirmation of feminine strength, since the ancients believed that girls were conceived on the left and boys on the right. She also was able to conclude, even though no ancient source said anything about it, that Amazon women did not make class distinctions among themselves, but all had equal access to power and opportunity.

In the treatise on matriarchy on which Diner based her reconstruction of Amazon society, Bachofen (1967, 147) started from the premise that mythology and legend preserve at least a nucleus of historical fact; or, to put it another way, that in spite of certain fanciful elements in one or another account, some record of an actual past is preserved. But this was to assume that the first narrators of ancient myth were interested in recording history or facts (as we think of them), rather than describing attitudes or similitudes or drawing moral lessons. In practice, it did not matter to most ancient writers whether they had actually seen or had access to an eyewitness account; they were concerned much more with describing enduring characteristics and establishing general truths about human experience. In the

Hippocratic treatise *Airs, Waters, Places,* the information about
the Amazons' life is included among a series of anecdotes that
explain why Asians are weaker, or more effeminate, than Greeks:
climate is one factor, environment another, since the Asians are
generally ruled by despots; then follows the description of the
Amazons and of the strange customs of the other Scythians.
Herodotus puts his account of the Amazons into a general
description of Scythia, 'a country no part of which is cultivated,
and in which there is not a single inhabited city' (4.97), a land
beyond the pale, with strange, interesting and occasionally
admirable customs that are in general demonstrably inferior to
those of the Greeks. It is important to note that in Herodotus'
account every feature of Amazonian society has a direct
antithesis in ordinary Greek practice. In ancient Greece, women
did not hunt or go to war; women's initiation rites did not involve
exposure to physical danger; women nursed their children and
stayed at home (Pembroke 1967).

Only two aspects of Amazon life are not inversions of Greek
ordinary practice, but are rather grotesque exaggerations of their
character derived from crude etymologies of their names. The
Greeks preferred to explain foreign loan words in their own
language, even at the cost of straining credibility. For example,
the story of being born from the sea foam (*aphros*) explains the
name Aphrodite (Hesiod, *Theogony* 195-6); her son is called
Aeneas because she had terrible (*ainos*) grief because of him
(*Homeric Hymn* 5.198-9; below, p.118). Accordingly, Amazon
was explained as *a-* (un- or no) *mazos* (breast); hence the story
that their right breast was removed. The tribal name
Sauromatae was derived from *sauros,* the Greek word for lizard;
hence the idea that Amazon mothers fed their babies not on milk
but on lizard juice. No ancient artist ever saw or even imagined
these practices, because the Amazons represented in art always
have both breasts.

Whatever we now might think of the positive values of
Amazon society, the Greeks treated them as negative
illustrations of what might happen if warrior women were in
control, that is, as a means of avoiding a dangerous hypothetical
situation that in fact did not exist. I say warrior women, rather
than simply women, because in myth and art their power
receives more emphasis than their sex. Several heroes fight
against them: Bellerophontes (on Pegasus) and the young Priam;

one of Heracles' labours was to bring back the girdle of the queen of the Amazons (Euripides, *Hercules* 408-18). Athenian vase-painters, when depicting this expedition, gave more credit to their own city's hero Theseus than to Heracles. Theseus was often depicted repelling an invasion of Attica by Amazons, who had come to claim their sister Antiope (or Hippolyte), who had been carried off by Theseus (Merck 1978, 101; Jacoby 1949, 895).

For all their strength and skill, the Amazons always lose their battles against male heroes, especially if they are Greeks. The Trojans have high hopes for Penthesilea and her friends, who arrived in Troy just at the time when the *Iliad* ends, but Achilles kills her on her very first day in the field (*Aethiopis* F 1/Q.S.I). Phidias' statue of Athena Parthenos on the Athenian Acropolis (now lost) had on the outer surface of its shield a relief of the battle of the Greeks against Amazons, and on the inside the battle of the gods against the giants (Pliny, *Natural History* 36.18, Pausanias 1.17.2). On the metopes of the Parthenon a battle of Greeks against Amazons was paired with the battle of Greeks against the monstrous Centaurs. On the temple of Apollo Epikourios at Bassae in Arcadia a frieze of Heracles fighting the Amazons was matched by a frieze of the Thessalian Lapiths fighting the Centaurs. In each case the Amazons are classified with the established enemies of law and order. In virtually every pictorial representation of conflict, the Amazons are shown being defeated; significantly, in Attic vase-paintings after 480 B.C., they are often shown in Persian costume, as if representing the great Empire twice defeated by the Athenians (Merck 1978, 103; Boardman 1982).

How historical were other ancient matriarchal societies? The evidence for their existence is equally unreliable (Cantarella 1981, 33-4). In her history lesson Lady Psyche also praises the 'Lycian custom', according to Herodotus unique among the world's peoples, of taking the mother's rather than the father's name and status (1.173). But Herodotus' account of the Lycians is not an eyewitness record; it simply represents the opposite of the standard practice of the Greeks. The same can be said about his description of the marvels of Egypt, where

the people, in most of their manners and customs, exactly reverse the common practice of mankind. Women do the marketing [in fifth-century Athens men or male slaves did the shopping]; men work the loom; women urinate standing up, men sitting down; daughters must support their parents; they write letters from right to left (2.35).

Here too he is not reporting the literal truth, but attempting to illustrate the foreignness of Egypt (Pembroke 1967, 1-18). For the Lycians also the other evidence we have suggests that maternity was no more significant for them than for other peoples. In the earliest reference we have to the Lycians, the Lycian Glaucus explains who he is by tracing the *male* lines of his ancestry (*Iliad* 6.196-210). His cousin Sarpedon is chief of the Lycians at Troy, rather than Glaucus himself, not because Sarpedon was the son of Bellerophontes' daughter, while Glaucus was son of his son, but because Sarpedon was the son of the king of the gods, Zeus (How & Wells 1912, i.134; Pembroke 1967, 29). Inscriptions from Lycia have recently been found that also reveal no trace whatever of a matrilinear system of descent (Pembroke 1965, 218-47; Vidal-Naquet 1970, 67).

Aristotle states explicitly that the 'Lycian custom' that Lady Psyche praises would have been interpreted by the Greeks as a sign of decadence; to Aristotle, the rule of women (or *gunaikokratia*) was a sign of how democracies tended to turn into tyrannies; women get out of hand, wives are permitted to inform against (i.e. get political power over) their husbands (*Politics* 1269b40, 1313b32). The Lycians, according to a summary of Aristotle's account of their government, 'are all pirates. They have no written laws, only customs, and have long since been under the rule of women. They sell false witness together with their property' (Heraclides, *Politics* 15 = Aristotle, fr.611.43 Rose; Pembroke 1967, 20). According to the third-century B.C. poet Apollonius of Rhodes, the Amazons also 'do not respect the laws of the gods' (*themistes*, 2. 987-8). Aristotle's pupil Clearchus (a contemporary of Apollonius) claimed that the Lydians could be considered decadent because they had been ruled by a woman, Omphale; she had been raped by Lydian men, and in revenge forced respectable women to have intercourse with slaves (Athenaeus 12.516a). This same Omphale was said to have purchased as a slave the greatest Greek hero, Heracles, and to have made him her lover (Scylax 709*FGrHist*F21; Pembroke 1967, 34).

Mythologies of matriarchy in other cultures serve a similar function. Joan Bamberger (1973, 268) has shown that myths about the rule of women from two culturally distinct areas are intended as negative examples. Both in Tierra del Fuego at the extreme south-west tip of South America, and in the tropical forests of the north-west Amazon and central Brazil women are said to have been the first to rule over the land and to have owned all the emblems of power; but they ruled without mercy and justice. Then, suddenly, in both myths the situation is reversed; the women are driven out, excluded from the secrets of power, and kept forever after subordinate. This changeover is also celebrated in ritual. The myths 'constantly reiterate that women did not know how to handle power when they had it'. They do not represent actual history but instead explain the way things are. 'The Rule of Women', concludes Bamberger (1973, 280), 'instead of heralding a promising future, harks back to a past darkened with repeated failures. If, in fact, women are ever going to rule they must rid themselves of the myth that states they have been proved unworthy of leadership roles' (cf. also Merck 1978, 108).

Greek myths of matriarchy, like the South American, are didactic rather than historical. But it is easier to accept that the Scuth American myths are unhistorical, because Greek authors present their material in such reasonable and rational form that it takes some time to realise how greatly their research methodology (if one can call it that) differs from ours. In the sixth century B.C. Greeks travelled to Themiskyra and the Thermodon River, on the south shore of the Black Sea, the land that in seventh-century B.C. epic poetry had been inhabited by Amazons; when they found no Amazons there, they did not give up their belief in the Amazons' existence, but rather thought of the Amazons as being located further away, in the part of the world that had not been explored, namely the uncivilised land of Scythia; other accounts put them in Ethiopia or places they had heard of but where no one had actually been. But as Pierre Devambez (1981, 642-3) has pointed out, if the Amazons had existed, other cultures would have represented them in their art; in fact only the Greeks seem to know about them. Nor have archaeologists uncovered the kind of empirical information that could confirm that Amazons, or female tribes like them, once existed. The Spanish explorers of Brazil named the great river they discovered there the Amazon because they saw native women fighting alongside their men (Kleinbaum 1983, 118); the discovery of fourth-century Sauromatian graves containing the skeletons of women and horses, with spears, may indicate that there were women warriors, but not that these women were independent of men, like the Amazons, or indeed matriarchal (David 1976, 130, 148, 151).

Since we are accustomed to think of Herodotus as the founder of modern history, it is difficult to appreciate how different the Greek view of reality is from ours. They thought in terms of probability (what they called *eikos*, what is fitting or likely), and did not distinguish between the remote or recent past, or accord more credibility to what could be demonstrated empirically than to what could be vividly described (even at third hand). In relating an account of a past event, an author was free to remove or add details to render his story more probable (Wiseman 1979, 143-53). This attitude has contributed greatly to modern confusion about the relationship of ancient myth and history.

For example, orators in fourth-century B.C. Athens spoke of the story of the Amazons' invasion of Attica as if it were as historical (in our terms) as the Persian invasion of 480. Athens' victory over the Amazons came to be regarded as her first major civic achievement. The orator Lysias in a speech for war dead in 389 (2. 4-6) depicts the Amazons as formidable enemies; they were the first to wear iron armour and to ride on horseback; they had conquered all their neighbours; but 'when matched with our Athenian ancestors they appeared in all the natural timidity of their sex, and showed themselves less women in their external appearance than in their weakness and cowardice'. All were killed on the spot. Other writers, less concerned with praising the state in general, described the battle in ways that explained the position of various monuments, such as the Amazoneum, various tombs, and a column outside the city gate near Phaleron commemorating the Amazon Antiope or Hippolyte, Theseus' consort, who according to some authorities was killed there, but according to others lived on to establish the Amazoneum at Troezen. Precise stategic and topographical details of the battle were supplied by Cleidemus, author of an early history of Attica, from his own imagination (Jacoby 1949, 75). Plutarch in his *Life of Theseus* (27) illustrates how an ancient author approaches his source material: he gives the most space to Cleidemus (323*FGrHist*F18), because of the detail his account provides. Plutarch adds other information when it corresponds to existing

monuments in Athens and elsewhere; he copes with contradic-
tions (such as when and where Antiope/Hippolyte died) by
giving both versions, and observes that 'it is hardly surprising
that history should go astray when it has to deal with events so
remote as these'.

Bachofen's approach to the evidence is no less eclectic than
Plutarch's, though his premises were more elaborate: he
assumed that myth represented if not a precise record of specific
institutions then at least a general impression of cultural
practice, enduring characteristics, and human psychology (1967,
150-1). Scholars in his day had become increasingly interested in
discovering the common grounds among civilisations of different
times and places. Artists like Wagner sought to recapture in their
own language and customs impressions of their vanished
heritage. Bachofen spoke of discovering in myth fixed and
recognisable laws, among them the notion that in primitive
societies woman could be seen to exert over man a powerful
religious and moral influence, so that even though she was
physically weaker, she was able to ensure the continuity of her
sense of social values. One suspects that his notion of ancient
realities was based on a contemporary appreciation of the role of
women in his own society, and that the fixed laws he saw in the
confused and contradictory record of the past were the patterns
he most wanted to find. His work had wide influence; Nietzsche
was familiar with it, and Engels adopted the idea of early
matriarchy because it gave support to the notion that the earliest
(i.e. natural) form of human existence had been communal
(Campbell 1967, l-liii; Cantarella 1983, 14-21).

Bachofen's theories would be of purely antiquarian interest
were it not that they continue to be taken seriously by scholars
who are not familiar with the methods of ancient historians. The
continuing appeal of his work results from his putting the blame
for women's loss of power onto male conspiracy, envy and
ignorance. By implication, then, restoring women to their
rightful place first of all requires recognition of that conspiracy,
and emphasis on whatever instances of female supremacy can be
discovered in past history, however remote in time or scattered in
different cultures. In 'The Princess', according to Tennyson's
narrator, Lady Psyche presented 'a bird's-eye view of all the
ungracious past' (ii.109), a survey in which she described events
in summary and out of context: women's status in the Persian,

Grecian, and Roman empires ('how far from just', 116); women
in China, Islam, the Age of Chivalry, and finally the present,
when 'commenced the dawn', and the future, with full equality
for women (162). Emotion is involved in every aspect of
academic discourse at Princess Ida's college: 'O lift your natures
up;/Embrace our aims; work out your freedom' (ii.74-5); the
faculty are more like clergy than professors in their desire to
convert and to retain a group of faithful.

Tennyson also makes it clear that in the process of recovering
events and of endowing them with a significance that they in fact
never had, Lady Psyche and her followers seem to have assumed
that because they are women they are competent to assess the
fate of other women in all of history and all over the world. But
better tools for the purpose, at least in the case of ancient Greece
and Rome, are knowledge of the languages and of the methods
and aims of ancient historical writers. Without this knowledge,
scholars run the risk of imposing present values onto the past,
and of writing not history but a new mythology.

Let me offer a few examples of the kinds of distortion that
result when scholars try to approach ancient literature directly,
as if they were reading the works of a contemporary writer.
Bachofen, relying in part on Aeschylus' *Eumenides*, claimed that
the discovery of paternity was a key factor in the shift from
matriarchy to patriarchy; he cites Apollo's famous lines that the
real parent of the child is the father, while the mother is merely a
vehicle for carrying the seed from which the child grows (658-61,
below p.122). Kate Millett, in her attempt to write a universal
history of the treatment of women in literature, not only
recapitulates Bachofen's argument in her discussion of the
Oresteia, but uses a rather free translation that seems to her
'closer in spirit to the original' because it puts special stress on
Clytemnestra's sexuality (1970, 111-15). But in the original the
argument about paternity, which no one in the audience would
have understood as a statement of general 'law' or truth, only
wins the day when the goddess Athena casts the deciding vote
(Winnington-Ingram 1983, 123-7), and in any case Clytemnestra is not just an ordinary woman, but a murderer by
treachery, 'who slew her husband, the watcher of the house'
(*Eumenides* 740). The female Furies who demand vengeance
against Orestes for killing his mother are not simply vanquished
by a new 'male' order; they are persuaded by the goddess Athena

to play a more positive role in the administration of justice by an offer of great honour, *timê*, which included material recompense in the form of sacrifice and powers, the sort of thing the Judeo-Christian divinities might not care about, but which no Greek god would ever disdain (Lloyd-Jones 1971, 4). Far from being suppressed, as Bachofen supposed, the Furies' great strength is recognised, since it is only with their support that Athens will maintain her judicial system and her political and economic importance (Winnington-Ingram 1983, 127).

But if it is assumed that women in antiquity were deprived of their original powers by a conspiracy on the part of men, and kept powerless because of men's fear that they would naturally try to reassert themselves, increased emphasis is given to the role of gender in myth, which seems even more plausible because of the importance given to the role of sexuality in the psychological theories of Freud. When Orestes in the *Eumenides* is purified by pig's blood, it has been argued that the pig's blood, by symbolic association with the female genitalia (a word for 'young pig', *delphax*, appears to be cognate with the root -*delph*, signifying 'womb'), represents a rebirth that breaks the original bond between the child Orestes and his mother Clytemnestra (Zeitlin 1978, 165-6). But in actual practice, outside the 'world' of this particular drama, pig's blood was used at Delphi to cleanse any murderer, not just matricides, of blood guilt (Lloyd-Jones 1971, 73; Parker 1983, 30n.66). In those many cases when the victim was not the murderer's mother, how could pig's blood have symbolised a rebirth that breaks the bond between the murderer and his victim?

Similarly, it is possible to view the myths of Amazons and other wild and destructive women who oppose men, like the women of Thebes in Euripides' *Bacchae*, as expressions of the psychological conflict imposed by the customary segregation of the sexes in Athenian society and men's apprehensions about female sexuality (Simon 1978, 250; Zeitlin 1982, 136). But myths of these conflicts, and rituals enacting them, existed long before and continued long after respectable women in Athens ceased to be confined primarily to their homes, and it is significant that in these myths not only the women, but the men who attack and pursue them suffer in the end from their violent behaviour. Nor does the defeat of the Amazons primarily represent the triumph of the male hierarchy over women, or express male sexual domination, simply because the Amazons are portrayed as young, attractive women, whom the men stab with their swords (cf. duBois 1982, 103; Tyrrell 1984, 42, 102, 113). If it can be argued that on the Parthenon metopes, which depict Theseus fighting against the Amazons in conjunction with the battle of the Lapiths against the Centaurs, the 'masculinised' Amazons represent *all* ordinary women, the half-equine Centaurs must be understood as representatives of *all* ordinary horses, and the Parthenon metopes thus must advocate the Athenian suppression of horses, animals that in reality were of course highly prized and well-treated.

Since the Greeks were perfectly capable of expressing complex meanings in both literature and art, there is no need to believe that if they wanted to say something about male domination of Greek females they could not have done so directly, without employing an 'ethnographical code' (cf. Tyrrell 1984, 59). The Amazons and other mythical women who attack men are destructive to themselves as well as to the rest of society; the myths' 'message' is directed both to women and to men, and warns that anyone who withdraws from or hates ordinary family life becomes dangerous to society as a whole. The Greeks, male and female, would have been surprised that Lady Psyche for her women's college chose the Amazons as 'emblematic of a nobler age', since to them the Amazons represented one of the best arguments for retaining a status quo in which groups composed exclusively of either sex were not permitted continuously to segregate themselves.

In the end, interpretations such as Lady Psyche's tell us more about ourselves than they do about the cultures that they purport to describe, rather like the anthropologists who failed to understand the purpose of the myths of the Trobriand islanders, and so deduced that the natives did not know where babies came from; imagine what those natives might conclude about our notion of sexual intercourse from a literal interpretation of the story of the Annunciation (Leach 1969, 85-112). How then should modern feminists try to approach the past, so that – to use Henry James' Olive Chancellor's phrase – 'men shouldn't taunt them with being superficial' (*The Bostonians*, 1886, ch.17)? We should, to being with, make a clear distinction between rewriting mythology, or, as Carolyn Heilbrun has called it, *Reinventing Womanhood* (1979, 157) and reporting history. In the latter case, we need to get beyond the stage of reaction, past Bachofen, Jane Harrison, and all the recent revivals of their work, back to the full texts of the sources they cite only partially, and back also to the kind of documentation Bachofen and his modern followers have not considered.

The social documents that will tell us most about the real status of women are to be found in places that few standard ancient history courses until quite recently considered: gravestones, boundary markers, wills, marriage contracts, materials found mostly on inscriptions and papyri; most are untranslated, most require special training to read, much cataloguing still needs to be completed. Studies of these documents in the last decade have begun to show that it is dangerous to derive our picture of the ancient world exclusively from literary documents, especially from dramas or legal orations, which portray the breakdown of normal life rather than its routine. In the fifth and fourth centuries B.C., Athenian members of Athenian families wished to be buried near each other, even when necessary moving established graves; in the fourth century details of their affection and relationship began to be described (Humphreys 1983, 79-130). Strong ties exist not only between mother and daughter but between husband and wife. Epic and drama themselves have much to tell us about normal relationships, if we look closely at what the characters say rather than simply at the main lines of mythic conflict. Upper-class women in all periods and places in the Greek world had the opportunity to be educated (Cole 1981, 219-45); if they did not voice dissatisfaction even in Rome, where women owned and managed property, perhaps they saw certain advantages in the status quo, such as protection and mutual trust. Lower-class women and women slaves lived in many respects the same kind of life as men, with set occupations and professions, some sex-segregated, but fewer than we might have expected.

The explanation of women's status will not be as easy to explain as Bachofen thought, and it may take several generations seriously to establish it, even for one small portion of the world's history, like ancient Greece and Rome. In order properly to evaluate these new findings, comparison must constantly be made with the status of men in the same period and country and equivalent social class. If I were asked what statues to put in front of the Wellesley College Library, I would not choose goddesses like Hestia and Athena, abstract paragons of what one can do if one is immortal, ageless, infinitely powerful; nor would I pick Amazons or the equally non-existent Lycian matriarchs, or even the swimmer Cloelia from Rome's legendary past. I would begin with some ancient women Lady Psyche had apparently never heard of, who won in their time the respect of their contemporaries, men and women both: the poet Erinna, composer of the epic poem the *Distaff*, about the death of a female friend (*Supp. Hell.* 401/*WLGR* 9); Hipparchia the philosopher, who travelled around lecturing with her husband Crates (Diogenes Laertius 6.96-8/*WLGR* 43); Menophila of Sardis, who was honoured by her city for being clever (she is shown with a book) and for being a leader (Peek 1881/*WLGR* 49); the philosopher Hypatia of Alexandria (below, pp.107-9). Certainly they were unusual, but they did exist – which we might not have guessed had we considered only the accounts of women in myth.

In the chapters that follow, rather than concentrate on myths about foreign cultures like the Amazons, where no historical documents can be adduced to gauge the degree of reality reflected in the myth, I want to consider some of the myths that deal with the role of Greek women, both ordinary and extraordinary, in central works of Greek literature. My approach will be to try to interpret these documents by comparison with other Greek or Roman texts, and with whatever documentary evidence as is relevant and available. Lest I be accused of lack of sophistication, let me assure the reader that I have resorted to this rather traditional approach not because I am unaware of the work of structural anthropologists, but because I prefer a method of interpretation that does not take our attention away from the language and emphasis of the original texts, and that does not attempt to describe complex human experience in the simplifying terms of polarities and oppositions.

2

Chosen Women

What would ancient Greek *women* have thought about Greek mythology? The ancients tell us very little about the process of their education, and in general we only know what male writers tell us women thought, because there are so few women writers. But certainly everyone, men and women, free and slave, knew the stories; in Euripides' *Ion* a group of slave women who have been brought to Delphi eagerly identify in the temple of Apollo the representations of gods, heroes and monsters which they recognise from stories that were told to them as they worked at their looms (196-7). In Athens everyone attended the theatre; as Plato puts it, dramatic poetry is 'a kind of rhetoric addressed to the general populace, including children, women and men, slave and free' (*Gorgias* 502d). Not that any woman (or man) would have regarded the stories of Oedipus and Jocasta or Agamemnon and Clytemnestra as 'norms', since they all belonged to a heroic past that no longer existed.

On the other hand, the myths place emphasis on the kind of experiences and problems – although in idealised or exaggerated forms – that most ancient women would encounter in the course of their lives. In myth, there were essentially two main courses of female existence: celibacy, or involvement with males and (inevitably) childbearing. The two states of course were mutually exclusive, though a woman (or goddess) could return to celibacy after her children were born. For mortal women, involvement with males was the more usual, and probably the more promising, alternative, since virginity offered freedom only to goddesses like Athena and Artemis, who as goddesses had the power to defend themselves and by definition were ageless and immortal. Virgin goddesses like Hestia and Hecate were

30

guaranteed protection and honour by Zeus. Other goddesses who had been wives or lovers of the gods could gain power temporarily by withdrawing from the males and by withholding something essential to men or to the gods; Demeter, for example, long since estranged from Zeus, won their daughter Persephone back from Hades by keeping the seeds of grain within the earth, so that humans began to starve and the gods got no sacrifices (*Homeric Hymn* 2.303-9). But to mortal women, who by definition as humans can be destroyed and will grow old, disengagement offered fewer rewards and posed greater dangers. Daphne refused to have sexual relations with Apollo and ended up fixed in one place, but as a laurel tree. Only in one respect does the existence of the virgin goddesses correspond to that of mortal women. Although the virgin goddesses were worshipped for their power over so many aspects of human life, they act only within limits defined by Zeus and with his approval, or with the co-operation of another god. Hesiod, in a passage that describes and virtually advertises a local cult, explains how Zeus honoured the virgin goddess Hecate beyond all others and gave her shining gifts (*Theogony* 411-12); *he* permits her to help or hinder kings, soldiers in battle, athletes in competition; with *Poseidon* she can help the fisherman (440-3), with *Hermes* the herdsman (444-7).

But myths about goddesses, and about women, concentrate on their relations with males, and most particularly on their first union with a male, which in the case of ordinary mortals at least, was their marriage. Hesiod's *Theogony*, the great epic about the origin of the gods, is a chronological catalogue of divine unions, in which the virgin goddesses like Hecate and Athena appear as rare exceptions; virtually every other goddess is the mother of children. Earth, who with her husband Heaven is the ancestress of Zeus, of the most important gods and of many primeval forces, asks her son Cronus to castrate his father because he hides all his children back in Earth as soon they are born, and she 'groans because she is oppressed' (160). But Cronus too swallows his children as soon as they are born, and so his wife Rhea has to devise a means of keeping one son, Zeus, away from him, so that Zeus can drive him out of power by force and rule over the gods himself. But Zeus prevents a recurrence of this cycle by having several wives and swallowing Metis, his first wife, so that he can bear Athena himself from his own head and thus keep her and her mother under his control (887-900). Then he has six other

wives, the last of whom is Hera, and many temporary liaisons
with both goddesses and women. Thus a patriarchal order is
established, with both women and children kept subordinate,
although with particular rights and responsibilities.

Hesiod does not say how Zeus tricked Metis ('Prudence') into
letting him swallow her, or note what she might have said when
she discovered that she had been tricked, but Homer in the first
book of the *Iliad* makes it clear that Hera very much resents
Zeus' granting favours to other goddesses, and opposing her
plans without consulting her (552-9). Hesiod in the *Theogony*
says nothing about the fate of Semele and Alcmena, the mortal
women with whom Zeus had relations; but later poets could
speak poignantly of both the perils and pleasures of intercourse
with a god. Perhaps the most vivid description of a union of this
type is spoken by Creusa in Euripides' *Ion*. Apollo had fallen in
love with Creusa but immediately abandoned her; years later, as
queen of Athens, yet unable to bear another child, she complains
that she can neither ask for the god's help nor tell her story
because even associating with a woman who bore a bastard child
might disgrace her. Like Persephone when she was carried off to
the Lower World by Hades, or Europa when she was approached
by a beautiful white bull who later turned out to be Zeus, Creusa
was gathering flowers when Apollo – his hair glittering with gold
– drew her into a cave, as she cried out in vain to her mother:

'You brought me there in shamelessness as a favour to the Goddess of
Love. And I in my misfortune bore you a son, and in fear of my mother I
left him in the couch where you compelled me, in misfortune, in my
sorrow, on a bed of sorrow.' (895-901)

When she speaks these lines she is angry at the god, who has – as
she believes – both abandoned her and failed to protect their son;
it is only after she attempts and fails to kill him that she
discovers that the boy her husband thought to be his son is in
fact her and Apollo's lost child, destined to be king of Athens.
Similarly, in the *Prometheus Bound*, after hearing the story of
Io's involvement with Zeus, and seeing her head horned like a
cow's and listening to her hysterical ravings, the female chorus
exclaims that they would not want to 'marry' one of the gods:

'Let my marriage be humble, may the passion of the powerful gods not
cast on me an eye none can escape; that is a war I could not fight, a

source of resourcelessness. I do not know who I would become. For I do
not see how I could escape the mind of Zeus.' (901-7)

Their words make it clear that they are afraid not only of the
gods' power, but of the physical changes in themselves sexual
union with a god might cause. A Hippocratic medical treatise
(*Virg.*, L viii 468) confirms that in the first stages of puberty (the
time when girls would ordinarily be married off), they became
hysterical and suicidal, like Io; the prescription and cure for
them is, as it was for her, pregnancy (Lefkowitz 1981, 14-15; King
1983, 114). Also, neither Io nor the chorus can see that for her, as
for Creusa, what she presumes to be misfortune will ultimately
bring her fame and happiness: the birth of a son who will be the
ancestor of a famous race, and whose descendants will include
another son of Zeus, Heracles.

Like Antigone, Io and Creusa are victims of *atê*, 'folly of speech
and a fury in the mind', because they do not understand the
consequences of their actions, and fear as a disaster what will
ultimately bring them fame and guarantee them a place in
history. Judged by standards of what Christianity promises to
the good, at least after the Day of Judgment, the Greek reward
for endurance may seem slight indeed. But in Greek religion no
human being, male or female, could live entirely without sorrow;
from Zeus' two jars of good and of evil, a person can get either a
mixed portion or *all evil*, but there is no possibility of *all good*
(*Iliad* 24.527-33). For women the best available 'mixture' would
seem to be marriage – however temporary – and family,
particularly if her children are heroes or the mothers of great
men.

Perhaps because the life of any individual human being was
perceived as being essentially temporary and fragile, the myths
tend to emphasise the importance of the continuity of the race –
not just of families, but of whole peoples. Creusa's son by Apollo
is Ion, ancestor not only of the Athenians but of the Ionians in
Asia Minor. Virtually every village and town claimed descent
from a god, often through a hero for whom the town was named,
as the Ionians were said to have been named after Ion. Hesiod's
Theogony ends with a long catalogue of marriages and
extra-marital unions between gods and goddesses, gods and
women, and goddesses and men, all of which result in the birth of
gods, goddesses, heroes and women who married heroes. Another

epic attributed to Hesiod, the *Catalogue of Women*, described the unions that produced all the famous heroes, nations and races; each new heroine was introduced with the words 'And like her was ... '.

For centuries we possessed only short quotations from the *Catalogue* and some prose summaries which could give little impression of the shape of the original epic, but in this century a number of long fragments were discovered on tattered strips of papyrus, and from these we can get at least a partial sense of the pacing and emphasis of the original narrative. Although Greek bards could describe brilliantly the excitement of sexual passion and the verbal and physical prelude to making love – the *Homeric Hymn to Aphrodite* is the best example – the *Catalogue of Women* seems to have been valued and recited, even in the Hellenistic Age, not for its power to engage the emotions, but as historical information, like the begats in Genesis or at the beginning of Matthew's Gospel, or the fascinating list of the different types of whales that interrupts the grim story of Melville's *Moby Dick*. The ancient Greeks seem to have been particularly fond of such catalogues – Book 2 of the *Iliad* contains a list of all the cities that sent ships and men to Troy (West 1985, 1-30). But Hesiod's catalogue attributes to women a significant role in this formal history. Each 'founding mother' is listed by name; none is merely an anonymous bearer of divine seed.

Like Hesiod's *Theogony*, the *Catalogue* is organised by genealogies, and within each family tree Hesiod concentrates on explaining why certain women captured the attention of gods or of heroes. In the first book Demodice (about whom virtually nothing is said in any other surviving text) is wooed by numerous suitors, as were Helen or Penelope, because of her 'unbounded beauty, but they didn't persuade her'. She held out, apparently, for a god instead, Ares, by whom she became the mother of Thestius, father of Leda, who in turn was the mother of the most beautiful woman in the world, Helen (fr.22MW). Mestra, daughter of Erysichthon, who had an insatiable appetite, was able to change into every type of animal; so each day her father sold her in exchange for food, and each night she changed back into human shape and returned to him, until Sisyphus bought her for his son and demanded arbitration when she ran away. But even then Sisyphus was not able to keep her, because 'Poseidon broke her (*edamassato* – the same verb denotes both

taming of animals and the taking of a virgin), far away from her
father in sea-girt Cos, carrying her across the wine-faced sea,
even though she was very clever' (*poluidris*, a term that always
seems to imply, both for men and for women, that one is tricky,
or too clever for one's own good; fr.43a.55-7). By Poseidon she
became the mother of the great hero Bellerophon (fr.43a.82-3).
Another fragment describes the contest for the athletic and
beautiful Atalanta (fr.73) from the point of view of her successful
suitor, Hippomenes:

The prize that awaited them both was not the same; swift-footed
god-like Atalanta raced refusing the gifts of golden Aphrodite; for him
the race was for his life, whether he should be captured (by Atalanta's
father) or escape: and so he addressed her with crafty intention,
'Daughter of Schoeneus, with your relentless heart, accept these shining
gifts of golden Aphrodite ... ' [He threw an apple on the ground] and she
snatched it swiftly like a harpy on delaying feet; but he threw a second
apple to the ground ... then swift god-like Atalanta had two apples, and
she was near the goal, but he threw a third to the ground, and with this
he escaped death and dark fate. He stood there catching his breath ...
(fr.76)

In these, and in every other case, the males win, which could be
interpreted as an illustration of the inferiority of women, if no
struggle to capture them were involved, and, as in Atalanta's
case, the women's skill were not so obviously superior. The
mother of a hero clearly must be more beautiful than other
women, but also cleverer or swifter than most men, and in the
end, can be subdued only by or with the assistance of the gods.
Perhaps the best example is Alcmena, the mother of Heracles,
the greatest hero of all. Her brothers were all killed, and she
'alone was left as a joy to her parents' – after which,
immediately, the next lines refer to Zeus, who wanted Alcmena
to be the mother of his greatest mortal son, Heracles (fr.193).
According to the epic *The Shield of Heracles*, another work
attributed to Hesiod but probably composed at least a century
later than the *Catalogue of Women*, Alcmena was more
beautiful, cleverer and (in our terms) sexier than anyone, and
also so faithful to her husband that Zeus had to pretend on her
wedding night that he was her husband. That occasion had been
postponed until Amphitryon had avenged the death of
Alcmena's brothers, but 'when [Amphitryon] had accomplished

the great deed he returned to his home, and he did not go to his slaves or the shepherds in the fields until he had gone up to his wife's bed – such great desire ruled the heart of the leader of the army; and he lay with his wife all night rejoicing in the gifts of golden Aphrodite' (38-41, 46-7), lest anyone (e.g. Slater 1968, 11-12) argue that Greek men got their sexual pleasure from extra-marital or homosexual relationships.

The moral superiority of women like Alcmena is significant, because the heroic age is brought to an end by the three daughters of Tyndareus, 'twice and thrice married and leavers of husbands' (fr.176/223*PMG*): Timandra who left her husband Echemus for Phyleus, Clytemnestra who 'after she deserted her husband Agamemnon slept with Aegisthus and chose a worse husband, and then Helen disgraced the bed of fair-haired Menelaus.' It is important to note that Helen, unlike Atalanta, is won not by the most daring man but by the man who offered the most gifts, and was not even present himself but rather was represented by his brother; the poet observes that 'Menelaus could not have won Helen nor would any other mortal suitor, if swift Achilles returning home from Pelion had encountered her when she was a girl; but before that warlike Menelaus had her, and she bore fair-ankled Hermione in his halls – though the birth had been despaired of' (*aelpton*, 90-5). At this point the gods were divided by strife, and Zeus wanted to destroy the race of men; the Trojan war followed, and with it, a kind of Heldendaemmerung: apparently, the race of heroes cannot exist without women of heroic calibre (95-103; West 1985, 119-20).

Since Greek myth glorified the role of mother, it also tended to condemn to infamy those who in some way rebelled against it. A confirmed mortal virgin who resisted the advances of a god might get away simply with metamorphosis into a tree or flower, but women who consciously denied their femininity, like the Amazons, or who killed their husbands and fathers, like the women of Lemnos, were regarded as enemies and monsters (Aeschylus, *Libation Bearers* 632-8). The expected outcome of any sexual encounter between a mortal woman and a god was a notable child – as Poseidon reassures Tyro both in the *Odyssey* and in the Hesiodic *Catalogue*: 'You will bear glorious children, since the embraces of a god are not fruitless' (fr.31MW, cf. *Odyssey* 11.248-50; Maas 1973, 66-7). But in the *Catalogue* when Poseidon had intercourse with the daughter of Elatus, king of the

Lapiths in Thessaly, and promised to grant her any favour she wished, she asked to be turned into a man, and to be made invulnerable (fr.87). This man, Caineus, proved to be a threat to the gods, because he did not respect the limitations of his mortality, like Ixion, who tried to seduce Hera, or Tantalus, who stole nectar and ambrosia from the gods to try to make his friends immortal. Caineus instead set up his spear in the marketplace and asked people to worship it, so that Zeus arranged to have Caineus' father's old enemies the Centaurs drive Caineus into the ground (fr.88). According to the prose genealogy of Acusilaus, Poseidon allowed the sex-change because 'it wasn't holy for them to have children by him or by anyone else' (2*FGrHist*F22=9B40aDK). If we compare the story of Thetis, whose son was destined to be greater than his father and who was therefore married to a mortal man, or the story of Metis, whom Zeus swallowed in order to produce her offspring Athena from his own head, the notion seems to be that by completely preventing rather than somehow mitigating the outcome of her pregnancy Poseidon makes Caineus dangerous and undesirable. Coronis, who has intercourse with another of Elatus' sons, Ischys, at the same time as she is pregnant with Apollo's son (fr.60MW=Acusilaus 9B39DK) is allowed to die, though the child Asclepius is saved only to be killed when he too oversteps mortal boundaries. Medea, who kills her children to get revenge on their father Jason, who has deserted her, gets away with her life, but knows she will live unhappily ever after. Clytemnestra, who helped to murder her husband Agamemnon in order to live with her lover Aegisthus, is murdered by her son by Agamemnon, Orestes; throughout the *Odyssey* her evil actions are contrasted with the faithful Penelope's. Modern women (e.g. Pomeroy 1975, 109) may admire these destructive women because they took action and used their great intelligence to right what they considered to be personal wrongs against themselves. But even the chorus of Corinthian women who at first sympathise with Medea's desire to punish Jason for deserting her, condemn the form that her revenge takes.

Even though so few options in life seem to have been available to Greek women (or men), the Greeks did not hesitate to give 'equal time' to description of the human dilemma, as seen from a *woman's* point of view. We can tell from the titles of lost plays that women were the central figures of many tragedies, as they

are in the ones that have come down to us. The poets, even
though they were men and though their plays were performed by
male actors, allow their female characters to describe their
predicaments in detail, as if they had been able to listen with a
sympathetic ear to the complaints of women in their own
families. Euripides shows with particular clarity how the
conditions of ancient marriage could be both restrictive and
frustrating. As Medea says, when a man is bored with his family,
he can go out and put an end to his heartache, but a woman must
stay behind, inside the house, and 'look towards him alone'
(Euripides, *Medea* 244-7). Phaedra complains of the aristocratic
wife's dilemma of having too much time on her hands to think,
and even of being with the man she loves but cannot have,
because of the disgrace adultery would bring not only to her but
to her children (Euripides, *Hippolytus* 373-430). Sophocles
depicts the plight of Heracles' wife Deianeira no less
sympathetically, abandoned year after year by her husband as
he goes about his labours and sleeps with other women; Heracles
sees his children 'like a farmer who sees a distant field only at
sowing-time and harvest' (Sophocles, *Trachiniae* 31-3). In a
fragment of his lost play *Tereus* the king's deserted wife
complains that women are happy only in their girlhood, in their
father's house, after which they are 'thrust out and sold to
strangers or foreigners, in joyless or hostile houses – and all this
once the first night has yoked us to our husband we are forced to
praise and say that all is well' (fr.583Radt=*WLGR* 32; Knox
1978, 312). Since Sophocles' and Euripides' dramas were
produced, often in competition with one another, throughout the
last decades of the fifth century B.C., from the beginning until the
disastrous end of the Peloponnesian war, all this time their
audiences were compelled to reflect on how their customs and
actions affected (or afflicted) women's lives.

It has recently been suggested (Slater 1968, 297-301; Girard
1977, 44; Foley 1981, 143; Zeitlin 1982, 131) that the destruction
of Athenian society was predicted in dramas like Euripides'
Bacchae, which describes how Pentheus, the king of Thebes, is
murdered by his mother in a Bacchic frenzy; the Greeks'
habitual misogyny compelled them to seek the company and
love of other men and to seek to restrict and repress the females
in their family. Euripides would then seem to be saying that if
women are confined to 'the loom and the shuttle' in the inside of

their houses, women will rebel and tear apart not only the fabric of their own weaving but of the family and the state; Dionysiac ritual thus provides a form of 'socialisation' that can keep the female under control (Zeitlin 1982, 136). But to judge from the emphasis in Euripides' text, I think it far more likely that both the poet and his audience saw in Pentheus' cruel death and the disgrace and exile of his mother a particularly vivid reminder of the universal power of *atê*, the deception which leads men to ignore the worship of the gods, and of the vital forces in nature which they represent, and of the 'folly in speech and fury in the mind' (Sophocles, *Antigone* 603) that will drive men to bring about their own destruction. Pentheus and his mother and aunts all refused to recognise the existence of the god Dionysus, and so the god whom they dishonour causes them to go mad and ultimately to destroy themselves. As in the *Antigone*, both men and women are equally subject to *atê* and both equally responsible for their actions. If Euripides suggests that if the women abandon their homes and infant children, and the responsibility of caring for the family that is represented by the loom, they will harm not only others but themselves, he is not recommending that women should enjoy the role that society has assigned to them, but simply that they accept it as the least destructive possibility; men too are compelled to play roles that they would not willingly choose – Cadmus, Pentheus' grandfather, had to abdicate his throne when he was too old to defend himself, and now must with difficulty try to pretend that he is young again in the ritual required by the god; at the end of the play, although he is an old man, and has done nothing himself to offend the god, he must leave the city he founded and end his days in the form of a snake.

Rather than insist that Greek men were misogynists because they did not give their women the 'equal rights' that women have yet to acquire even in the most advanced democracies of this century, I would suggest that they be regarded as pioneers in recognising and describing with sympathy both the life and the central importance to their society of women. Women, to whom their society assigned the task of lamenting and burying the dead (Garland 1985, 29), are very often in the position of being the last commentators on the war or murders described in an epic or a drama, and male poets did not hesitate to allow them to make articulate and poignant observations about the futility of all that their men had prized so highly. They assume an important role in drama because they are passive and are required to remain at home or away from the scene of the action, natural victims, and thus are able to represent the human condition, man's true powerlessness before the gods and the fact of his own mortality (Lefkowitz 1981, 1-11).

But even though male Greek writers of the fifth century B.C. were capable of such brilliant description of the problems of women's life, they were not equally good at offering solutions. Even the philosphers of the fourth century B.C. were better at explaining how the world worked than at proposing any *practical* change. In the Hellenistic period, when the Macedonian conquests had imposed more efficient governance and caused Greek culture to come in contact with new ideas, the law, centuries behind the facts as always, granted women in name some of the rights they had already had in practice, but despite greater physical comfort and freedom of movement, women's basic role in life was unchanged (Pomeroy 1985, 120, 154), and the old myths continued to be told and retold, even by the best and most sophisticated court poets in Alexandria. Medea, in Apollonius' epic *The Voyage of the Argo*, has the run of the palace and, with her handmaidens, of the city of Colchis, but she is still dependent on her father, and then on her lover Jason; the destructive powers of her magic and her selfish desires lead to her exile, the death of her brother and unhappiness for both Jason and herself.

At least by stressing the importance of the family and of women's role within it as nurturers and continuers of the race, the Greeks attributed to women a vital function that the Church Fathers were later to try to deny them, when they placed an even higher value on the state of celibacy and offered to virgins a new subservience rather than increased independence (below, p.129). Comparison with narratives about women in the early Church reveals that the Greeks – however immoral their tales were from the point of view of Christian ethics – at least placed a higher value on women's initiative and intelligence. In Luke's Gospel, Mary is chosen to be the mother of God's son because she is a virgin; thus fulfilling the prophecy in Isaiah (7.14), 'Behold the maiden (*parthenos*) shall conceive in her womb and she shall bear a son, and they shall call his name Immanuel' (Matthew 1.23; Harvey 1973, 19). We hear nothing about any of her other qualities, though she does, in the course of the narrative, display both piety and common sense: 'How can this be,' she asks, 'since I know no man' (Luke 1.34). The sexual encounter that invariably marks the culmination of the episodes in Hesiod's *Catalogue* is of course missing in Luke: 'The Holy Spirit will come to you and the power of the highest will overshadow you' (1.35); instead the incident emphasises the power of God: 'And behold, Elizabeth your kinswoman, she has also conceived a son, in her old age, and this is the sixth month for her who had been called barren' – and here the angel cites Genesis 18.14 – 'because "nothing at all will be impossible for God" ' (1.36-7). But in Greek mythology gods choose women because of their distinguished genealogy – Io, for example, was the daughter of the river Inachus – or for their beauty – even Cassandra, whom we remember because of her ability to prophesy accurately, was the 'most beautiful of Priam's daughters' (*Iliad* 13.365), or for their courage – Apollo sees Cyrene wrestling alone with a lion (Hesiod, *Catalogue* fr.215), or for their intelligence – Poseidon finally outwitted the 'very clever' Mestra (fr.43a55-7).

Of course I do not mean in any way to deny that from a modern point of view the patterns of women's experience described in Greek myth are severely limited; but then we cannot really blame them for not having been able to envisage the advantages for women that the industrial and scientific revolutions would bring. At the same time it would be foolish to claim that these old patterns have lost all their influence, or even appeal. If feminists now seek to concentrate instead on those relatively few myths and authors whose heroines assert themselves, even if only to hasten their own or others' deaths, that is to be expected, and possibly even applauded. But it should be stressed that the original myths, with their original emphases, also have something to teach us; *atê* is still with us, and perhaps nowhere more obviously than in the belief that the ambitious career woman can 'have it all', without divine intervention, or at least the creation of new narrative patterns that help to chart some of the crises other than marriage and childbearing that may arise as the result of her longer and more complex life. In addition to reminding us of the limits of human vision, the ancient texts also emphasise the importance of 'nature' as opposed to 'nurture' in human life, and suggest too in their concentration on certain critical moments that in other respects as well human existence is perceived episodically, even though it is lived chronologically. But perhaps the most important notion that Greek mythology has helped to fix in our minds is that women have not only the right but the power to comment on the events that shape their lives, even if they cannot control them; and because they have a voice, they are able to speak not only for themselves, but for humankind in general.

3

Women without Men

Myths describe only certain segments of an ordinary span of life. Others, including some periods which we now consider particularly significant in the course of human development, seldom or never appear in even the most extended narrations. We meet the women in Hesiod's *Catalogue* at the moment when the god sees them, or at the time of their marriage to a mortal man; or in the case of Alcmena of both at once:

She came to Thebes with warlike Amphitryon, daughter of Electryon protector of the people; she surpassed all other women in appearance and height; and no one could contend with her in intelligence of all the women whom mortal women bore after intercourse with mortal men. (*Shield* 2-6).

Of her girlhood we hear nothing, except, in the *Catalogue* (fr.193.19), that she was the only child left 'as a joy to her parents' after her brothers were killed. But the poet does not describe the effect of this tragedy on her adolescent mind. We learn how she feels only by her actions as a bride: she loves and honours Amphitryon more than any wife ever honoured her husband (*Shield* 9-10), but she refuses to sleep with him until he has avenged the death of her brothers (*Shield* 14-18).

Exceptional women like the warrior Atalanta or the huntress Cyrene are not really exceptions, for we learn about them only when they are old enough to be married. Atalanta stops to pick up the apples that Hippomenes drops for her and so loses the race and becomes his bride (fr.76); Apollo is drawn to Cyrene because of her courage, when he sees her wrestling alone with a lion (fr.215, quoted by the scholiast to Pindar, *Pythian* 9.6,

II.221Dr.). Before she lost the race to Hippomenes, Atalanta
killed two Centaurs who tried to attack her; she was one of the
participants in the hunt for the Calydonian boar, and there met
the hero Peleus, who wrestled with her and was defeated by her
at the funeral games of Pelias (Apollodorus 2.9.2). Vase-painters
liked to portray their match, no doubt because wrestling in
antiquity, as now, had obvious sexual connotations (Poliakoff
1982, 104-5; Bernardini 1984, 113-14.) In other myths,
heterosexual wrestling serves as a prelude to intercourse. Peleus
had to wrestle with and defeat the goddess Thetis before he could
marry her and beget Achilles (Pindar, *Nemean* 4.61-4;
Apollodorus 3.3.5; Frazer 1921, 2.67). Apollo fell in love with
Cassandra, who, according to Homer, was the most beautiful of
Priam's daughters (*eidos aristên, Iliad* 13.365), and as Aeschylus
has her describe it in the *Agamemnon*, 'he was a wrestler
(*palaistês*) who mightily breathed his grace on me' (1206). In
other words, he attempted to make love to her (by 'grace', *charis*,
she means what we might call sex-appeal), but, as she says, 'I
gave my consent and then I played him false' (1208). As his part
of the bargain, Apollo had given her the gift of prophecy (1210).
When she broke her promise his revenge was to keep her from
ever being believed (121; Fraenkel 1962, iii.555).

Of course women, like men, had childhoods, and occasionally
a poet in the course of a narrative will describe young girls. When
in the *Homeric Hymn to Demeter*, the goddess, grieving for her
lost daughter, sits down in mortal form beside the Maiden Well
at Eleusis, she is discovered by the four daughters of the king of
Eleusis, Celeus: 'They came after the water that was
good-to-draw, to bring it in bronze jugs to the dear home of their
father, four of them, like goddesses in the bloom of youth,
Callidice and Cleisidice and lovely Demo and Callithoe, who was
the oldest' (*Homeric Hymn* 2.106-10). They ask the old lady who
she is, and when she says she would be willing to work as a nurse
in their household, Callidice, who is not the oldest, but the most
beautiful (*eidos aristê*), answers her (146). Then they run home,
after filling their jugs, to get their mother's permission, and
return to the goddess: 'they leapt like deer or calves in the
springtime in meadow, satisfying their appetites with food, so
they ran, holding the folds of their lovely clothes along the hollow
wagon-road, and their hair streamed about their shoulders like
the crocus flower' (174-8). The contrast between the lively young

girls and the sedentary mourning goddess is most effective. But even this delightful description suggests some of the limitations of the lives of young girls: for safety, they went out in groups, and only to public places, though even at wells girls might be accosted. They use their intelligence, but of course must ask for permission before taking action. By contrast, the old woman 'who is excluded from childbearing and the gifts of Aphrodite who loves garlands' (101-2) is safe although sitting alone. Sexuality, or perhaps more accurately, sexual vulnerability, determines the degree of freedom or mobility a mortal woman can have (Bremmer 1986).

For this reason, when a god wishes to rape a mortal woman, he has to devise a way to remove her from her home or from the group of girls with whom she would ordinarily travel. The myth of the rape of Persephone provides the model. At the beginning of the *Homeric Hymn to Demeter*, Aidoneus snatches Persephone

... when she was playing apart from her mother Demeter of the gold sword, of the shining harvest, with the deep-bosomed daughters of Ocean, gathering flowers, meadow and iris and hyacinth and the narcissus, which Earth made to grow as a snare for the maiden with eyes like buds, in accordance with the will of Zeus, marvellous, and bright, a thing of wonder to all who saw it, immortal gods or mortal men ... it sent forth such a sweet scent that the broad heaven above and all the earth laughed and the salt swell of the sea. And she then in wonder reached out with both hands to take the beautiful plaything. And the earth with its wide ways opened in the Nysian plain and the lord, Receiver of Many, rose up to meet her with his immortal horses, the son of Cronus who has many names. (4-18)

Later in the poem, when Aidoneus sends her back to her mother, Persephone tells Demeter 'all of us were in the lovely meadow, Leucippe and Phaeno and Electre and Ianthe, and Melite and Iache and Rhodeia and Callirhoe' – she lists twenty-three names in all, including at the end 'Pallas, rouser of battles, and Artemis delighting in arrows' (417-24). The catalogue seems intended to assure her mother that in such a large and formidable company she could ordinarily have expected to be safe. Indeed, in another version of the myth, so well-known in Euripides' time that it needed no elaboration, 'swift as the whirlwind they rushed after her, Artemis with her arrows, and, in her armour with the Gorgon's face, Athena with her spear' (*Helen* 1314a-16; Kannicht 1969, ii.342-3).

The techniques employed by the gods in the rape of Persephone recur in stories about Zeus and mortal women. To seduce Europa, who like Persephone was gathering flowers with her friends, Zeus changed himself into a bull, and as an outline of the *Catalogue* puts it, 'exhaled the scent of saffron from his mouth' (fr.140). Hellenistic accounts add details that make the bull sound if not attractive, at least magical, intriguing and deceptively harmless, like the narcissus flower (e.g. Moschus 2.79-107). As Io tells her story in the *Prometheus Bound*, Zeus resorts to dreams that urge her to leave her maiden chamber and go alone to the wide meadow of Lerna to meet him (647-54). The poet of the *Catalogue* seems not to have described Europa's reaction, but rather to have concentrated on the compensation given to her father: 'she crossed the salt water ... conquered (*dmêtheisa*), by Zeus' tricks ... and Father Zeus gave her a gift that Hephaestus famous for his craft made with knowing intelligence and took to her father; and he received the gift' (fr.141.1-6). But the author of the *Homeric Hymn to Demeter* emphasises that Persephone was unwilling and miserable (19-20):

She cried out loud and called on her father (21).

As long as Persephone saw the earth and the flowing sea with its fish and the rays of the sun, still she hoped to see her dear mother and the family of the immortal gods ... the tops of the mountains and the depths of the sea resounded with her immortal voice, and her goddess mother heard her, and sharp pain seized her heart.(33-40)

The poet makes it clear that Persephone is not so much frightened by Aidoneus as by the thought of being separated from what was familiar to her – a fear particularly real in her case because she literally will be taken away from the world of light and life to dwell beneath the earth with the dead. Europa, on the other hand, was only taken across the sea from Phoenicia to Crete and sent to live with the king Asterion (fr.140). None the less, other poets realised that a young girl's reaction to such sudden change might equally well be terror. In the *Prometheus Bound*, Io recalls how Zeus tried to get her to come outside alone so that he could seduce her:

Visions at night kept coming to my maiden chamber and saying with entreating speeches, 'O greatly fortunate girl, why are you remaining a maiden so long, when it is possible for you to have the greatest marriage? Zeus is inflamed for you by the arrow of passion ... My child, don't despise the bed of Zeus but come out to the wide meadow of Lerna, to your father's sheepfolds, so Zeus' eye may be relieved of longing.'(647-54)

The dreams neglect to explain precisely how *she* will profit from the experience, and she does not respond until an oracle comes directing her father to drive her out of his house, 'against his will and hers' (663-72)

Homer indicates that Nausicaa has extraordinary presence of mind when she alone remains to confront the naked Odysseus, 'who seemed terrifying to them [Nausicaa's companions] because he was fouled with salt, and they fled trembling one after the other to the wagons' (*Odyssey* 6.137-8), and Odysseus knows what to say to reassure Nausicaa, 'a gentle and crafty speech' (148). But Electra in Euripides' play is immediately suspicious when she sees strange armed men before her house. She tells the women of the chorus, 'You flee down the road and I will avoid these evil men by running into the house.' (218-19).

The myths give the impression that while a young woman can freely associate with other young women and their own fathers and brothers, any encounter with an extraneous male is potentially dangerous. Clytemnestra in Sophocles' *Electra* complains that her daughter 'is running around loose as usual outside the house', because her step-father Aegisthus is not at home to restrain her from 'disgracing her family' (516-18). Creon decrees that both Antigone and Ismene must 'now be women and not range about outside' (*Antigone* 578-9). Since fifth-century dramatists portray young girls' seclusion as normal, at least in the heroic age that their plays describe, it is tempting to think that Athenian girls – at least of the upper classes – also led such protected lives. Menander seems able to assume that his audience too will take it for granted that no respectable girl ought to go out alone. When in the *Dyscolus* Cnemon's daughter meets a young man on her way back from the well and he offers to draw water for her, Cnemon's old slave, who sees them talking, naturally assumes that the young man is planning to seduce her and blames Cnemon for failing to provide her with an attendant:

'I don't like this at all. A young man looking after a girl! It's no good. Cnemon, I hope the gods almighty destroy you. You let your innocent daughter go alone into the countryside without anyone to guard her. Probably the boy found out about it and sneaked up, thinking it a rare stroke of luck.' (218-26)

The slave then goes off to get the girl's brother. The situation was the same in rural modern Greece. Whenever a girl

goes out on some errand to gather firewood or carry water, she has a companion go with her. In the popular mind wells and illicit sexual intercourse are linked together. If a man for any reason wants to see the local girls he has only to sit by the well and by and by he will see them all. (Campbell 1964, 86)

In fact the young man in the *Dyscolus* has fallen in love with Cnemon's daughter, but his intentions are honourable. Although love-at-first-sight may be primarily a convention of romantic comedy and of novels, its existence in so many plots suggests that young men and women of marriageable age were kept segregated as much as possible, and that myth accurately reflects the importance of virginity, or to put it the other way round, of certifiable paternity.

By concentrating on the moment a girl catches a man's eye, the myths seem to be implying that motherhood is a woman's most important destiny, and her first encounters with men more significant in emotional terms than any other experience of her childhood. In these stories, the outdoors seems to mark the first stage of separation of the child from her family, as well as the first involvement with the unfamiliar, in all senses of that word. Thus it appears that aside from this first and irreversible break, ancient girls were not perceived to have the developmental problems that even the smallest infants are believed to experience in our society, from the trauma of birth to the first awareness of sexuality, in the period of latency, pre-teen anxiety and the stress of menarche. For ancient women, the only one of these problems that counted was menarche, and that in large measure because it coincided with betrothal and marriage. The writer of the Hippocratic treatise *On Virgins* observes that if young women become hysterical it is because the blood in the womb has no place to flow out and so backs up and adversely affects the other organs; the cure, naturally, is to widen the egress from the womb by intercourse with a man and pregnancy (*Virg.*, L viii 468, above, p.31). If there were other problems peculiar to young girls, neither the myths nor the medical treatises focus on them.

But of course the myths in the forms they have come down to us were written by men, who did not necessarily have either the inclination or the opportunity to observe what women felt or thought when they were away from them. The author of the *Homeric Hymn to Demeter* describes women (and goddesses) talking to each other, though only in response to the rather extraordinary situation of the story. Still, we can glean from their conversations a sense of women's strong affections and sympathy for one another and their concern for the relationship between mother and child. The goddess Hecate, herself a virgin, hears Persephone's cries and comes to tell Demeter about them, and then goes with her to ask Helios, who sees all, for more information. Celeus' daughters and later their mother Metaneira comfort the old woman they meet at the well, much as Achilles comforts Priam or Nausicaa reassures the wretched Odysseus, by reminding her that men must endure what the gods give (Richardson 1974, 226). An old woman, Iambe, 'with kind intentions', gives Demeter a seat and cheers her up by telling her jokes (194-205). When Demeter in anger abandons the baby Demophoon, his sisters come to the rescue: 'one took the child in her arms and held it on her lap, another re-lit the fire, a third rushed on gentle feet to revive her mother' (285-7). When Persephone and Demeter are reunited, Hecate stays beside them and embraces Persephone, and Rhea, Demeter's mother, comes to persuade her daughter to rejoin the company of the gods.

The devotion of Demophoon's sisters to their mother and their brother, and their kindness to the old lady they find at the well, along with Metaneira's anguish over the treatment of her only son, help to express in terms of mortal experience what the goddesses Demeter and Persephone feel when they believe they are to be separated permanently from one another. Of course, by definition, goddesses cannot die, but Demeter's reaction, when she hears Persephone's cries, resembles closely the responses of Hecuba and Andromache when they see that Achilles has killed Hector and has begun to mistreat his corpse (Richardson 1974, 161). When Hermes brings Persephone back from the lower world, 'as soon as she saw her Demeter rushed towards her like a maenad along the mountainside shadowed by forest, and Persephone opposite jumped down and ran ... ' (385-9). The

simile of the maenad, which in the *Iliad* is used to describe
Andromache when she is afraid that Hector has been killed in
battle (6.389, 22.460), here also may signify fear as well as joy,
since Demeter immediately asks Persephone the question that
will determine whether or not they can be permanently reunited,
whether she has eaten anything when she was in the world below.

It is this reunion of mother and child, with the promise of its
renewal each year, that marks the climax of the poem, and that
is meant to offer hope to all men by its celebration in the
Eleusinian mysteries. Demeter gets Persephone back, though she
is not quite the same Persephone, and only for a portion of the
year. Yet they accept this compromise gladly: 'for the whole day
with one spirit (*homophrona thumon*) they soothed their hearts
and spirits with embraces and their spirits ceased from
lamentation; they received joy from one another and gave it back
in return' (434-6). There is a striking contrast between the
goddesses' rejoicing and the description of human existence at
the end of the *Iliad* where, as Achilles says, men must live in grief
while the gods are without care, and the best a man can get from
the two jars on Zeus' threshold is a *mixture* of evil and good
(24.525-30). Did the Mysteries – the rites of initiation into the
cult of Eleusis – suggest that in reunions of parent with child,
Persephone with Demeter, Demeter with Rhea and the other
gods, lies the secret of the continuation of life, not so much the
life of the individual, but of the race? Demeter, when deprived of
her own child, immediately seeks to nurse another, and it is this
act, and the kindess the young girls show her, that eventually
leads to her partial recovery of her own child and, though the
hymn – perhaps deliberately – does not say how, to the birth of a
new child, here called Ploutos, 'Wealth', who according to
Hesiod is the son of Demeter and a mortal man, Iason, with
whom she had intercourse in a ploughed field (*Theogony* 971;
Richardson 1974, 316-17). Thus mothers' love for their children
and women's role in sustaining life are in various, mutually
reinforcing ways fundamental to one of the most important and
long-lived cults in the ancient world.

Grave inscriptions suggest that women in real life also were
remembered primarily for their role in the family. Scenes with
women and children are frequently depicted in funeral sculpture
and on vases (e.g. Ampharete; Hansen 1983, no.89; Kurtz 1975,
56, pl.42.1), but perhaps the clearest expression of the

importance of the role of wife and mother may be found in the memorials left explicitly to those who were denied it. In the sixth and fifth centuries, there are many fewer memorials to young women than to young men. Since it was the custom to avoid personal details and to stick to essentials, it is the more striking that parents chose to add that their young daughters had never been married: Phrasicleia (*c.* 540 B.C.) is represented on her tomb as saying, 'I shall be called a maiden always. This is the name the gods gave me instead of wife' (Hansen 1983, no.24=*WLGR* 21; Humphreys 1983,153; Gressmair 1966, 63-75). In tragedy, of young girls who are about to die it is said that they marry Hades, or, less vividly, that a funeral is to be substituted for their wedding – a convention that indicates why an ancient audience would have been moved by the portrayal of Demeter's grief in the *Homeric Hymn* (cf. Euripides, *Iphigenia at Aulis* 461; *Medea* 985; Sophocles, *Antigone* 654, 816; Euripides, *Hecuba* 416, 612; Kurtz & Boardman 1971, 161). The same notion is occasionally applied to boys (e.g. Euripides, *Heracles* 480-2; Lattimore 1962, 193), but in the poems of the Greek Anthology, which preserve conventional thoughts in their most polished form, only *girls* are said to marry death (Gressmair 1966, 75-7). It could be argued that these sentiments represent primarily a man's view of the value of a woman's life, as in the case of the husband who complains that Hades is less discriminating than himself in his choice of wives:

Nico, the lawful wife of Archon; but Hades has carried her off, who does not take any account of evil or of good. But she was clever and blameless; her husband placed her here with his own hands when she died, the Cretan daughter of Aristocles, a double sorrow, before the pious woman could bear fine children. Let someone else marry a wife like her with a happier fate, a wife who knows how to manage a sound household. (Peek 866, 3rd century B.C., Alexandria)

But since several of the epigrams in the Anthology were written by professional *women* poets, like Anyte and Erinna, we may perhaps assume that women regarded a girl's untimely death with much the same regrets as men:

I weep for Antibia, a virgin. Many suitors wanted her and came to her father's house, where she was known for her beauty and cleverness. But

fate sent all their hopes rolling away. (648GP=*WLGR* 12=*AP* 7.490;
Lattimore 1962, 194 n.62; cf. *FGE* 678ff.)

The only women who are seen to express different notions about
their primary role in life, or are seen to complain of it, are the evil
women of epic and tragedy, who bring destruction on their
families and on themselves, like Clytemnestra, Deianeira and
Medea. But perhaps it can be argued that if women, rather than
men, had written these works, we might have found more
support for other, or at least more varied, roles. It is certainly
true that male poets, so far as we know, did not describe intense
emotional (and physical) attachments between girls in the same
age-group (*helikia*), such as the ones Sappho describes in her
poems:

'The truth is, I wish I were dead.' She left me, whispering often, and she
said this, 'Oh what a cruel fate is ours, Sappho, yes, I leave you against
my will.' And I answered her, 'Farewell, go and remember me, for you
know how we cared for you. If you do forget, I want to remind you of
violets you set beside me and with woven garlands made of flowers
around your soft neck ... and with perfume ... royal, rich ... you
anointed yourself and on soft beds you would get rid of your desire ... '
(94LP=*WLGR* 5).

In another poem, another girl has left Lesbos and now

is unique among Lydian women, as the moon once the sun sets stands
out among the stars, and her light grasps both the salt sea and the
flowering meadows and fair dew flows forth, and soft roses and chervil
and melilot bloom. Often as she goes out, she remembers gentle Atthis,
and her heart is eaten by grief. (96LP=*WLGR* 5).

Has the girl gone off to be married? or has she simply gone back
home after being trained by Sappho to dance in the chorus?
Whatever the context of the original poems, their language and
situations were adapted by later poets to express the most
extreme manifestations of *heterosexual* passion. The poet Erinna
speaks with eloquence of a childhood shared with a girl friend
and of the sorrow the death of this friend – just after her marriage
– has brought her (*Suppl.Hell.*401=*WLGR* 9). But it is
impossible to say whether these isolated voices represent what
ordinary girls felt about one another, or whether they simply

demonstrate how (especially in Sappho's case) a great poet can endow the transient experience of adolescent friendships with lasting significance.

When 'good' women in Greek epic and tragedy are seen in conversation with one another, they do not speak of their lost childhood or friendships with other girls, but of the family. But even though their behaviour represents what men – if not they themselves – would desire, male poets should at least be given credit for allowing them to play important roles, and to make the final, and perhaps most sensible, judgments about the value of the male world.

Poets starting with Homer portray women as the survivors of the wars men fought for and around them, and as such allow women to make the final judgments on human achievement, judgments in most cases that would surely be different from men's (Lefkowitz 1981, 1-10). Not that Homer meant Andromache's view of war to override or negate Hector's; in the text both views coexist, although in an irresolvable tension, and for that reason it would seem that the Greeks *did* care to represent what women thought, and even •in works about war sought to give their view prominence.

Women attain heroic stature in epic and drama by managing through suffering to understand and to endure. Hecuba or Andromache attain prominence as characters in epic and drama; but it would be wrong to infer that the characteristics of women's heroism are exclusively feminine, or that women, in their turn, could not achieve 'heroic' stature for taking aggressive action. As Winnington-Ingram (1982, 247-9) has recently pointed out, Sophoclean women, especially Electra and Antigone, are ready to assume the initiative, and to express to men and women alike a degree of hostility and anger worthy of an Achilles. But women in the myths are for the most part placed in positions where they are powerless to effect any change, and for that reason the poets often chose them to represent the condition of mankind in general (Wiersma 1984, 54-5).

Euripides uses the same character, Hecuba, to describe both the active and passive forms of 'heroism.' In the *Hecuba*, Hecuba endures the loss of two of her children and then deceives her son's murderer and avenges his death by having her women slaves blind him and kill the murderer's two sons. In the *Trojan Women*, Hecuba simply endures one sorrow after another. She

comments in the course of the drama on a series of actions taken
by others, but because she is mortal she cannot see that her
advice and observations will prove to be correct. At the end of the
play she wishes that she could die in Troy, in contradiction to the
advice she gave earlier on to Andromache that living, even in
slavery, was better than dying: 'Death is not the same as being
alive; for death is nothing, but in life there are hopes' (631-2).
When she gave that advice, she had only seen her daughter
Cassandra led away to be Agamemnon's concubine and learned
that her daughter Polyxena had been sacrificed on Achilles'
tomb. By the end of the play she has seen Andromache carried
off, Menelaus unable to kill Helen, and her grandson Astyanax
thrown from the walls. But the audience knows that she will die
near Troy and that she will soon be avenged, because they have
heard Poseidon promise to 'stir up the Aegean sea' so that the
Greek fleet will be scattered, and they have heard Cassandra
prophesy that Agamemnon will be murdered on his return.

For this reason the *Trojan Women* cannot really be considered
a 'Peace Play', though it has long been fashionable to think of it
as a counter-cultural statement, expressing the horror of a
pacifist playwright at the war crimes committed by the
Athenians in Melos, and his sympathy for the Melian women
and children who were sold as slaves after the Athenians had
killed their men (cf. Vellacott 1975, 163-6). Certainly Poseidon's
warning at the end of the prologue is meant to have a general
application: 'Any mortal is a fool who destroys cities and temples
and tombs, the shrines of the dead; when he gives them over to
destruction he himself perishes afterwards' (95-7), but it is a
warning to soldiers who commit impiety, like Ajax son of Oileus
who raped Cassandra in Athena's temple, not to soldiers who
carry out the cruel but necessary work of subduing a potentially
dangerous enemy. Hecuba and all the women in the play are
helpless, but by no means complacent. Cassandra reminds
Hecuba of the past achievements of the Trojans who have died
honourably in war, and claims that by her marriage she will
destroy those whom she and her mother most hate – a boast that
the herald Talthybius only permits because he believes her to be
insane. Andromache accuses the Greeks of having invented evil
barbarian practices because they wish to kill her innocent son,
and suggests that they wish to dine on his flesh, as if he were a
human sacrifice, and Hecuba later adds a mock epitaph that the

Greeks killed him because they were afraid of him, 'a disgraceful inscription for the Greeks' (1191-2). The killing of Astyanax was a crime far more serious than anything the Athenians are known to have committed in the action against Melos, where the children were not murdered but enslaved (Thucydides 5.116.4); the Greek legal formula 'children and women' emphasises the higher priority given to children (Weidemann 1983, 163-70). Hecuba says to Andromache before she knows that Astyanax is to be killed:

> Honour your new master, and give him a good indication of your character, and if you do this, you will make friends for the common good, and you could raise this child to be a great hope for Troy, since children born from you might resettle Ilium again, and there might be another city. (699-705)

This possibility of regeneration is one of the 'hopes in life' that Hecuba tells Andromache about; once again we see women advising each other and, indirectly, all of us, about their crucial role in the survival of the race.

Because men and women both regarded mothering as woman's most important role, anyone who wished to make fun of women would portray them as being preoccupied with adultery and abortion. Semonides, in his satire on women, says that only the bee-woman, the one good kind out of a total of ten types, 'takes no pleasure in sitting among women in places where they tell stories about love' (fr.7W, 90-1, tr. Lloyd-Jones 1975; cf. Menander *Dyscolus* 381-9). Hippolytus, hardly a sympathetic observer, insists that women instead of slaves should have dumb beasts to live with them, 'so that they could neither speak to anyone or get a reply from them in turn' (Euripides, *Hippolytus* 645-8), since presumably every slave would behave as a go-between, like Phaedra's old nurse. But when poets allow us to eavesdrop on women's conversations, especially in the elegant little epic poems that were meant to offer to literate Hellenistic audiences impressions of ordinary life, women are seen chatting about a variety of subjects, mainly practical. Some concern men, like Herodas' mime about the old procuress who wants a *hetaira* to take a new lover (Herodas 1=*WLGR* 108), or substitutes for men, like the woman who wants to find out where to buy the best dildo (Herodas 6=*WLGR* 109). Some women complain about their husbands' insensitivity and inefficiency:

He brings me here to the ends of the earth, and gets me a hovel, not a house, so that we can't be neighbours, out of spite, envious brute, he never changes ... Just the other day I said to him, Daddy, go and buy some soap and rouge at the booth, and he came back with salt, the big ox. (Theocritus, *Idylls* 15.8-10, 16-17)

Women paying a visit to the temple of Asclepius admire the sculptures for their verisimilitude: 'Look at this naked boy; if I scratch him, he'll bleed, won't he, Cynna?' (Herodas 4.59-60). Most of these women complain about the laziness and stupidity of their slaves, everyone's greed but their own, and all go back home again at the end to their husbands: 'Dioclidas hasn't had his dinner; he's all vinegar, don't go near him when he's hungry' (Theocritus 15.147-8). Their conversation can be banal, selfish and trivial, but then, so can a man's, even when he is talking about love; the Cyclops, pining for Galatea, remarks that he seems to himself to be good-looking, when he looked into the sea, 'but to avoid the evil eye, I spit into my lap three times' (Theocritus 6.39-40).

According to the comic poet Aristophanes, when women gather at the festival of Demeter Thesmophoros, they hold a formal meeting to indict Euripides for making men think that they behave like Stheneboea and other disreputable females in his dramas. The most outrageous 'revelations' about adulteresses in action are made (as we might expect) by a *man* dressed as a woman, who concludes: 'And don't we all do these evil things? By Artemis we do. So then why are we angry at Euripides, when we are getting only the punishment that we deserve?' (517-19). But it would be foolish to mistake this entertaining parody for a serious description of what actually happened at ordinary Thesmophoria, when women met without men present. No one, of course, thought it worth recording what the women said to each other, just as they did not record what anyone, male or female, said during the actual procession to Eleusis or in any other ritual celebration. What mattered was the eternal, the continuation of the ritual itself. And if we trust a particularly astute observer of the purpose of ancient cult, the third-century poet Callimachus of Cyrene, the point of the Thesmophoria was to ensure Demeter's continued protection of human beings and of crops. Callimachus of course only saw and explained what women did in the public part of the festival:

As we walk through the city without sandals and with our hair unbound, so we shall have our feet and hands unharmed forever. And as the basket-bearers bring baskets full of gold, so may we acquire boundless gold. The uninitiated women may proceed as far as the city hall; the initiated right to the goddess' temple – all who are younger than sixty ... (*Hymn* 6.124-30)

What did the initiated women do and say inside the temple? We know from Aristophanes that the women prayed to the two goddesses and to Ploutos (295-6) and that in the rites at Eleusis at least, there was some celebration of the birth of Ploutos, as the *Homeric Hymn to Demeter* suggests: 'Blessed is the mortal whom the two goddesses eagerly love; they will then send Ploutos to dwell with him in his great house, Ploutos who gives wealth to mortal men' (486-9; Richardson 1974, 26-8). We know that at Eleusis at least Demeter was encouraged to eat, and thus to renew her care for human life, by Iambe's telling her jokes (203), an event that was commemorated in the ritual jesting of the Eleusis festival. Since it is very likely that these jokes were indecent (Richardson 1974, 214), once again the evidence seems to suggest that women were in private, as in public, primarily concerned with the process of becoming wives and mothers.

Nor does the information we have about other rituals celebrated by women suggest that any of these occasions were used to protest about women's role or the way the men were running the world. When in Aristophanes' *Lysistrata* the herald complains that the orator Demostratus' requests to the Assembly for ships for Sicily and men for Zacynthus were interrupted by his wife's lamentations for Adonis, he is merely complaining that women are notoriously self-indulgent (*exelampen hê truphê gunaikôn*), and can't abandon their amusements to pay attention to the serious business of the men (136-44, cf. Pherecrates 170K). At this festival, as Sappho describes it, the women lamented not their own fate, but Adonis' short life and the brief span of his romance with Aphrodite: 'Gentle Adonis is dying, Cytherea, what should we do? beat your breasts, maidens, and rend your chitons' (fr.140LP; cf. Pherecrates 170K). Part of the appeal of the story lay in Adonis' age; he was young enough to be a son, but old enough to be a man: 'His beard is still downy, so his kiss doesn't scratch' (*Theocritus* 15.130). The celebration itself provided opportunity for flirtation. In Menander's *Samia*, a young man explains how he was able to observe the Adonia:

Since the festival provided much opportunity for fun, as usual, I was present, alas, as a spectator. The noise inspired in me a certain wakefulness; I carried some gardens up to the roof; the women were dancing, and went off separately to celebrate all night. I hesitate to say what follows. I guess I'm ashamed. It's no use. But I'm still ashamed. The girl is pregnant. (41-9)

The gardens he mentions consisted of seeds planted in pots that grew quickly and died, like Adonis himself (Detienne 1977, 109-10). So it seems that the Adonia, like the Thesmophoria, were concerned primarily with the continuation of life:

Dear Adonis, the story is that you alone of the gods come here and go to Acheron ... be favourable, dear Adonis, and come again next year. You have made us happy by coming this year, and when you come again, you will be welcome. (Theocritus 15.136-44)

The lamentations for lost girlhood in women's poetry may have a function analogous to the ritual for Adonis in that they help place particular experience into a general pattern, and enable women to prepare for a major transition in their lives. Homosexual experience is in one sense a preparation for heterosexual experience; the same goddess, Aphrodite, offers satisfaction in both, and in Sappho's poem (fr.2) we cannot tell whether the sleep that comes down from the rustling leaves in the temple-grove of Aphrodite follows fulfilment from hetero- or homosexual relationships. In Alcman's *partheneion* (fr.1*PMG*), the singers state that it is the leader of their chorus who arouses them (*teirei*, 77), but at the same time they describe her in ways that would appeal no less to men: Hagesichora is like a horse among the herds, strong, prize-winning, with thundering hooves, a horse of the world of dreams (fr.1, 45-9; Calame 1977, ii. 69-70). Cyrene catches Apollo's eye when she is wrestling with a lion; Atalanta had defeated Peleus and was able to run faster than any man when she was caught by Hippomenes' trick with the apples (Hesiodic *Catalogue* fr.43A, above p.35). It is of course at the moment when a woman seems most singular even to other women that she most appeals to men. Sappho relates in her poem about the girl who went away, 'now she is unique among Lydian women as the moon when the sun sets stands out among the stars', whose light makes the meadows bloom (fr.96. 6-14=*WLGR* 5, above p.52).

If one of these outstanding women managed to avoid the god's eye, or persuaded her father not to marry her to a mortal man, what could she expect to do for the rest of her life? For goddesses, virginity guaranteed independence, but goddesses had the power of Zeus to defend their immunity from the works of Aphrodite. Two of the virgin goddesses are concerned with what was ordinarily man's work. Athena deals with wars and the work of Ares, conflicts and battles and glorious works; she first taught mortal carpenters to make war-chariots and chariots worked with bronze (*Homeric Hymn* 5.8-13). Artemis enjoys bows and arrows and slaughtering wild beasts (16-20). Both Athena and Artemis also share in women's activities, like weaving (14-15) and dancing (19-20), and other virgin goddesses have existences that more closely resemble mortal women's. Hestia is allowed by Zeus, in exchange for marriage, to sit in the midst of the household as well as in all the temples of the gods, and to take the fat from the hearth (29-32). Hecate, according to Hesiod, like Demeter, has control over the fertility both of humans and of the earth, and also over the success of men's livelihoods (*Theogony* 416-49). But human virgins, because they are mortal, have no supernatural protector and will grow old, have none of these powers or privileges. Artemis can stand head and forehead above all the nymphs of the field, so that her mother can rejoice in her heart and she herself can be easily recognised, but if Nausicaa, whom Homer likens to Artemis, had encountered a god or even a man less honourable than Odysseus, what would she have been able to do to defend herself? (*Odyssey* 6.105-8).

For a mortal woman, maintaining celibacy required keeping a low profile, staying in the crowd of other women, doing women's work, like the several unattached females who took refuge from the war in the house of their relative Aristarchus, who could not afford to feed them, until Socrates advised him to put them to work, as one would female slaves (Xenophon, *Memorabilia* 2.7=*WLGR* 105). An old woman, as we have seen in the story of Demeter, can go about by herself. The priestess of Apollo at Delphi, an old peasant woman, can go outside alone, as we see her at the beginning of Aeschylus' *Eumenides*. But she too is helpless in an emergency, 'an old woman afraid is nothing, no better than a child' (38, tr. Lloyd-Jones 1982). Presumably a virgin or old woman was chosen to be Apollo's priestess because it was necessary for her to be completely subject to him, like a

wife, in order to be able to prophesy. Cassandra, who would not
submit, was of course doomed not to be believed. For the Vestal
Virgins also, virginity was a form of service as well as of reward
(Plutarch, *Numa* 9-10), as for the goddess Hestia/Vesta herself,
in exchange for marriage. As the Lemnian woman discovered,
when they murdered their sons and husbands and sent the king
off their island, they could run the country for a while, but
literally and figuratively could not manage long without men:
they needed an army in case of invasion, they needed children
once the young women began to grow up, they needed someone
with the strength to plough the fields (Apollonius of Rhodes,
1.675-6). No ancient author, male or female, fails to attribute to
women their share of intelligence, but none suggests that it is
possible or desirable for women to adopt any pattern of existence
other than those traditionally assigned to them, or, to put it
another way, to live in a world without men.

4

Wives

If recently feminist writers have placed too much emphasis on the restrictions and limitations of ancient women's lives, at least they have provided some compensation for the apologetic and uncritical estimations made before the civil rights movement of the 1960s (Gould 1980, 39-42). These earlier studies had tended to single out the accomplishments of certain exceptional women; they tended also to leave the impression that, since most ancient women do not appear to have complained about the kind of lives they led, they regarded the customs and laws that governed their lives as equitable and natural. Not that one should assume from the existence of extraordinary achievement that most women found such roles attainable or desirable; virtually all the ancient women who accomplished something notable were aristocrats, and almost always related to an important man. Artemisia of Halicarnassus the sea captain (Herodotus 8.87-8=*WLGR* 40) and Cynna the Illyrian strategist (Athenaeus 13.560f.) had 'professions' because their fathers were kings. Cynisca of Sparta in the early fourth century B.C. claims to have been the first woman to have won the four-horse chariot race (*AP* 13.16=*WLGR* 44), but then she too was daughter of a king; another female chariot-race winner was Bilistiche, the hetaera (or mistress) of Ptolemy Philadelphus, king of Egypt (*POxy* 2082=*WLGR* 46; Pomeroy 1985, 20). If women like Sappho and Corinna were able to be poets, it is in large measure because women could compose verse at home without moving outside the ordinary routine of women's existence. Aristocratic women in all periods composed poetry: the Argive poet Telesilla was said to have studied music because she was sickly (Plutarch, *Moralia* 245c=*WLGR* 39); we have a papyrus fragment of Erinna's epic poem 'The Distaff' (*Supp. Hell.* 401), and epigrams by several Hellenistic women are preserved in the Greek anthology.

But is it really fair to assume, as some of us have done, that the majority of ancient women would have wanted to emulate these accomplishments, had they had the opportunity? In this chapter I would like to examine in detail several documents in which it is possible to discern some of the positive aspects of conventional life. To begin with, we had better ask from a man's point of view what kind of women's behaviour wins praise. The basic categories are clearly set forth in Semonides' celebrated satire (fr.7W=*WLGR* 30). In this poem, as so often, the good is defined primarily by means of the bad. The one laudable type of female, the bee woman, is described after a list of eight despicable women, and since the bee woman herself is followed by reflections on women's deceptiveness, the poet leaves the impression that a good woman is (to say the least) exceptional, because she occupies only 11 of the surviving 118 lines of his poem:

Another is from a bee; the man who gets her is fortunate, for on her alone blame does not settle. She causes his property to grow and increase, and she grows old with a husband whom she loves and who loves her, the mother of a handsome and reputable family. She stands out among all women, and a godlike beauty plays about her. She takes no pleasure in sitting among women in places where they tell stories about love. Women like her are the best and most sensible whom Zeus bestows on men. (83-93, tr. Lloyd-Jones 1975)

Some of this positive description is expressed in negative terms: 'On her alone blame does not settle' (84) and then 'she takes no pleasure in sitting among women in places where they tell stories about love' (*aphrodisious logous*). Also, except for the phrase 'She grows old with a husband whom she loves', nothing is said about how *she* feels; the rest is stated from her husband's point of view: she causes his property to increase, he loves her, she has fine children; she stands out among all women (the phrase implies heroic stature). If such women are judged best and 'most sensible', it is because their lives are dedicated to serving their husbands and maintaining their households. It is significant that the bee woman is praised for not talking with other women about sex, first because that would encourage infidelity, and secondly because it would take her away from work or even send her outside the home in order to meet with other women.

It is easy enough to understand from Semonides' poem why her husband loves her, but why does *she* love her husband? Since the only woman poet we know about who was roughly contemporary with Semonides – Sappho – did not write poetry about women's affection for men, we must turn to poetry by men for information. I suggest that we begin with Penelope and Alcestis; they are the archetypes of good women, at least according to a husband in a fourth-century B.C. comedy, who can only come up with those two names to set against a long list of bad women (Eubulus, fr.116,117K=*WLGR* 34). Penelope conforms to Semonides' negative criteria: she remains faithful to her husband for twenty years, despite constant temptation; she stays in her rooms in the palace, except for brief public appearances when she is accompanied by maids or her son Telemachus. She does not associate with other women (except for the female slaves who attend her). Everyone acknowledges that she is superior to all other women, particularly for her intelligence:

Skill in exquisite workmanship, a keen mind, subtlety – these she has beyond anything we have heard of even in the ladies of olden times ... not one of these had the mastery in devising things that Penèlope has ... (2.116-22, tr. Shewring 1980)

This description, which is offered by the suitor Antinous, suggests that hers is a special kind of intelligence, involving plotting and planning that seem to men devious because they cannot immediately understand it. As Semonides said, 'In the beginning the god (i.e. Zeus) made the female mind separately.' But Penelope uses her particular intelligence to remain faithful to her husband, first by tricking the suitors for three years by unravelling at night the shroud she was weaving (in Antinous' words, 'a trick that went beyond all reason', 2.222) and then by testing Odysseus to see if he really is her husband, by pretending not to know the secret of the construction of their marriage bed (23.177ff). Certainly by the end of the *Odyssey* we understand why Odysseus was willing to give up Calypso and a promise of immortality to return to Penelope, even though, as he says to Calypso, 'I know that my wise Penelope, when a man looks at her, is far beneath you in form and stature' (5.217). But why does Penelope wait for Odysseus?

In part, it is because Odysseus, as Penelope herself says, was 'peerless': 'His fame has gone through the length and breadth of Hellas and Argos' (1.344). In part also, it is his house, which he himself helped to build, 'a house so beautiful and so filled with treasures, a house that sometimes, I think, I shall remember, though it be only in my dreams' (21.77-9). But there is also the matter of reputation: she wonders, 'If I should stay with my son and keep everything unchanged, my estate, my waiting-room, my lofty-roofed house itself – respecting my husband's bed and the people's voice' (19.524-6). As she says after she has recognised Odysseus: 'There was Argive Helen, child of Zeus; never would she have lain with a foreign lover if she had but known that the warrior sons of the Achaeans were to carry her back again to her own land' (23.218-21). Helen's action was wrong because it caused suffering and death for so many; Penelope also calls it 'folly' (*atê*, 222) because it seems clear to her that Helen would not have left Menelaus had she been free to remain; as Homer shows in Book 4, Helen has no complaint about her life with Menelaus after the Trojan war in his fine house in Sparta. It is possible to infer from Penelope's remarks that a woman has reason to be faithful if her husband is a person entitled to respect, and if she herself is well-treated; certainly both she and Helen, because of their husbands' wealth and position, live in security and comfort.

What else does Penelope expect (and get) from Odysseus? First of all, proof that she in her way is as important to him as he is to her. She does not demand strict fidelity; neither she nor Helen object to their husbands' liaisons with other women, so long as they are temporary; Odysseus tells Penelope about Circe and Calypso; Menelaus is able jointly to celebrate the marriage of Hermione, his daughter by Helen, and of Megapenthes, his son by a slave woman (4.4). But, as her questions about their bed indicate, it is important that they sleep together; also that he tell her immediately what he knows about his future plans, since that will affect both of them. Odysseus listens to her describing her experiences with the suitors before he tells her about his journey. But Penelope does not question his right to tell her what to do, or seek to persuade him not to set out again for new battles and journeys, since it is success in these that defines his importance in the world, and to her, because she counts on him (in a society without police and law courts) to protect her against their many enemies.

Alcestis, at least as Euripides portrays her, lives in a world that is not presently threatened with human violence; yet her attitude toward her husband Admetus is much the same as Penelope's to Odysseus. She is, of course, classified as 'good' because she offered to die in her husband's stead, when no one else, not even his aged parents, would volunteer. Euripides' drama takes place on the day of her death; like John of Gaunt in *Richard II*, she speaks portentous last words on stage, but Euripides also conveys to us her more private thoughts, by having one of her women slaves report to the chorus what Alcestis said in her own quarters, before she comes out of the palace for the last time to be seen by the community at large. These private words and actions conform to the pattern of behaviour that society (to judge from Semonides) would approve. She washes and dresses in special clothing (like Socrates before he drinks the hemlock, in consideration for the women who must prepare her corpse for burial). Then she prays that her children both make good marriages and live full lives; she sees that the appropriate myrtle boughs are placed on the altars; all this calmly, without shedding a tear. But even when she does break down and cry, her thoughts are for her husband, her children and her household. First she addresses her marriage bed: 'Here I lost my maidenhood to this man, on whose behalf I die; farewell, I don't hate you; you have destroyed only me, for since I was reluctant to betray you and my husband I am dying. Another women will possess you; not more chaste, but perhaps more fortunate' (177-82). Then she throws herself on the bed, weeping, and walks about the room only to throw herself on the bed again; her children cling to her, and she embraces them; all the slaves are weeping, but she gives her hand to each and speaks to every one of them, even the most lowly. In all this time she does not confide specially in another woman, not even a sister or a nurse; her sorrow, like Penelope's, is private, and we learn of it only at second hand.

Alcestis' public appearances, like Penelope's, are conducted with dignity and control. After she is carried outside, she addresses Admetus and reminds him of the reasons she decided to die for him, but again without complaint. She could have lived and married another king, but she did not want to live without him, with orphaned children, since she had had 'all she needed to be happy' (289). Nor did she want to deprive his parents, who were too old to have children, of their only son. She asks Admetus only one favour, not to marry again, because she does not want to have a stepmother for her children who would wish to put her own children ahead of them (305-7). She is not asking him to be celibate or not to take a concubine, but specifically not to acquire another legitimate wife, and Admetus himself readily agrees 'even in death you will be called my wife' (329-30); it is testimony of his remarkable devotion to her that at the end of the play he is reluctant even to accept a concubine, when Heracles appears to be offering him one.

In a society like ours, where male and female lives have under the law at least an equal value, Admetus might seem unduly selfish because he allows Alcestis to die for him. Some (Smith 1960, 127-45) have even sensed hypocrisy in his request to her, 'Do not betray us' (202, 250, 275), even though that is what survivors might say to the dead person on grave inscriptions (e.g. 'You rush off to the gods, Domnina, and forget your husband' Pleket 26=*WLGR* 171). But it is important to note that Alcestis, even behind the scenes, is never represented as having hesitated over or complained about her decision. Admetus himself does not question her decision until after his father has accused him of murder and cowardice and Alcestis herself has been placed in her tomb; then Admetus admits that he now understands (*arti manthanô*, 940) that he will be unhappy without her wherever he goes; that he can't bear the thought of another woman, or the criticism that he was a coward. Some scholars have interpreted this speech as a confession of guilt, but Admetus never says that he thought he should have died, just that now Alcestis is dead he does not want to go on living, which is quite a different matter.

Aside from the practical reason (in terms of Athenian inheritance laws) that in his family Admetus was the only surviving son who could serve as guardian of family position and property, why does Alcestis readily agree to die for him? Euripides could have chosen to portray her as a morbid, impulsive psychotic, but instead he makes it clear that her decision was undertaken deliberately and rationally. Like Penelope, she would have been able to marry again: 'I could have the man I wanted from among the Thessalians and live with a ruler in his prosperous home' (286). When she says she had from Admetus everything she needed to make her happy, we can assume that Admetus at least fulfilled the basic roles of protector and provider, and Euripides also shows us in the drama that he was justly renowned for his hospitality and generosity. Whether these qualities were in themselves responsible for Alcestis' devotion to him, Alcestis herself does not say; but her dialogue with him indicates that she trusts him to do as he promises, and her actions when she is alone inside the house show that she is reluctant to leave the marriage bed that (in her words) 'has destroyed' her (179). It is possible that she was afraid that a second time she might be less fortunate – as Medea puts it, 'everything depends upon whether you get a bad man or a good one' (235-6); but Alcestis, even in her soliloquy, says nothing like that, nor does she speak (as a Puritan woman might) of doing her duty.

Euripides apparently could count on his audience being able to believe that married couples could be as devoted to one another as Admetus and Alcestis; inscriptions from gravestones indicate that such sentiments were at least conventionally expressed, if not actually felt. There is, for instance, the inscription on a fourth-century B.C. stele that shows a woman holding out her hand to her husband, with verses that awkwardly represent a dialogue between them:

Farewell, tomb of Melite, a good (*chrestê*) woman lies here. Your husband Onesimus loved you and you loved him in return (*philount' antiphilousa*). You were the best (*kratistê*), and so he laments your death, for you were a good woman. And to you farewell, dearest (*philtate*) of men; love (*philei*) my children. (Kaibel 79=*WLGR* 26)

Alcestis' last request is virtually the same. Admetus implores her: 'Lift up your head, don't leave your children.' Alcestis replies: 'I wouldn't if I could help it; children, farewell' (388-9, cf. 302-3)

It is understandable that children would provide the principal reason for a married couple's devotion to one another. But even when there are none, or their presence seems to be unimportant, strong ties of affection exist, and even sexual attraction (though some contemporary scholars imply that ancient Greek men had little physical interest in their wives (Gould 1980, 56-8). In the *Suppliants* Euripides describes Evadne and Capaneus virtually as lovers. She refuses to abandon him in death (*prodousa*, 1024, the same word Admetus used of Alcestis), and throws herself on

Capaneus' funeral pyre: 'I will join my body to my husband in the burning flame, placing my beloved flesh next to his' (1020-1) ' ... hallowed is the bridegroom who is softened by the guileless attraction [lit. 'breezes', a word that denotes a sudden, powerful sensation] of his noble wife' (1029-30).

There are indications that similar devotion existed outside the context of the ideal marriages of myth, even in the ordinary marriages arranged by Athenian fathers for their children. In a fragment of a lost comedy, a young husband who thinks his wife has betrayed him explains that 'since the night I was married ... I haven't been away from bed a single night, away from my wife ... I wanted (*êrôn*) her, honestly ... I was tied to her by her noble character and her unaffected ways; she loved me (*philousan*) and I cared for her (*êgapôn*)' (Sandbach 1972, 327=*WLGR* 36). Three of the Greek words for love occur in this passage, *erao*, denoting sexual passion, *phileo*, love for family and friends, and *agapao*, affection. In his commentary on this fragment, Hugh Lloyd-Jones (1964, 28) observed that this appears to be the only instance in extant Greek literature where the three words 'recur at such short intervals, in each case referring to love between a man and a woman, and indeed between a husband and a wife'; but it is possible that if more literature about ordinary life had survived, the concurrence even in the context of marriage of all forms of love would no longer appear unique.

Another papyrus fragment indicates that a wife can display extraordinary affection for a husband who seems to lack what we might have deduced from myth was the single most important male virtue – wealth. The fragment preserves part of a speech by a wife to her father; she is begging him not to take her away from her husband, who is bankrupt, in order to marry her to a richer man:

Explain to me how, by whatever he has done, he has done me wrong. There is a covenant between man and wife; he must feel affection for her (*stergein*) always till the end, and she must never cease to do what gives her husband pleasure. He was all that I wished with regard to me, and my pleasure is his pleasure, father. But suppose he is satisfactory as far as I am concerned but is bankrupt, and you, as you say, now want to give me to a rich man to save me from living out my life in distress. Where does so much money exist, father, that having it can give me more pleasure than my husband can? How can it be just or honourable that I should take a share in any good things he has, but take no share in his poverty? (Sandbach 1972, 328-30=*WLGR* 38)

Since the rest of the play is lost, we do not know anything about this wife's circumstances other than what she tells us in this speech; here she is deferential to her father, and disparages her own intelligence, and suggests that perhaps only in the case of her own affairs a woman may know what is right. To judge from her own words, much of the 'pleasure' she derives from marriage comes from obedience and an opportunity to serve; also she makes it clear that her husband has been good to her in respects other than financial.

This wife's attitude reflects a new emphasis – at least in drama – on human relationships. Among families with property, marriages had been arranged primarily to ensure the safe transmission of property: a man in his will could leave his wife to a freedman or a daughter to a close friend; if a man died without male issue, his daughter was required to marry his closest male relative, even if that man had to leave his wife to do so. Euripides in his *Andromache* demonstrated that marriages arranged for political or financial purposes could be less than successful: 'A sensible man will arrange to marry children from a noble house to noble people, and not have any desire for base marriages, not even if they bring vastly rich dowries to his house' (1279-82). The devoted wife in the papyrus fragment, instead of discussing inheritance laws, speaks of 'a covenant (*nomos keimenos*) between man and wife; he must feel affection for her always, till the end, and she must never cease to do what gives her husband pleasure.' The Greek word *nomos*, here translated as 'covenant', is usually translated 'law'; but *nomos* does not so much denote a law in our sense of the word, i.e. a statute or the carefully documented precedent of. court decision; *nomos* is rather 'practice', and so may be expressed differently in different cases. The *keimenos nomos* or enduring practice that the wife here describes positively is expressed in tragedy in negative terms, and we can understand what she means by 'a husband must always feel affection for his wife' by comparing how Hermione and Deianeira complain that their husbands have ignored them and given a wife's status to a concubine: 'Husbands who want to live in a happy home show affection (*stergousin*) by keeping their eyes on one Cypris [i.e. sexual relationship] in their marriage' (*Andromache* 179-80). In reply to Hermione, Andromache describes the second half of the covenant, how 'a wife must never cease to do what brings her husband pleasure': 'A woman must, even if she has been given in marriage to a poor man, feel affection (*stergein*) for him, and not hold a contest of wills' (213-14); 'It is not beauty, but excellence that makes a husband happy' (207-8 *terpousi*). Andromache claims that she 'shared' Hector's sexual misadventures with him (*sunêrôn*), and often nursed his bastards herself, so as not to show him any bitterness, 'and by so doing I won my husband over by my excellence'. Euripides' Andromache is perhaps exaggerating in order to emphasise the justice of her cause against Hermione – in the *Iliad* it is the priestess Theano, not Andromache, who brings up her husband's bastard son 'in order to please him' (5.70). But still a wife had no choice under the law (or *nomos*) other than to be tolerant of her husband's sexual relations with other women, so long as her status as wife was recognised. As for deference to her husband's will, the wife in the papyrus fragment illustrates that this is the *nomos* by her insistence that her father knows best, and must decide, even though she does not agree with him. That she is able to express her point of view within the context of that *nomos* suggests that the heroines of tragedy, like Andromache or Alcestis, are not stepping out of line when they politely, but eloquently, speak to the men in their families. The male speaker of Lysias' orations recounts how a widow not only knew the terms of her husband's will, but was able effectively to argue before her male kinsman how her own father had failed in his duties as guardian (32.13-18).

These passages from drama and comedy suggest that more upper-class women at least managed to express themselves and influence their male relatives under Athenian 'law' or *nomoi* than a simple restatement of the laws, as they are expressed in trials or treatises, would lead us to believe (Gould 1980, 50; Cole 1981, 234). Law by nature emphasises prohibition and so fails to stress the positive; the arguments for chastity, for example, are always stated negatively 'if she breaks the law (by committing adultery) she wrongs the gods of her family and provides her family and home not with its own offspring but with bastards. She wrongs the true gods, etc ... she wrongs her own fatherland because she does not abide by its established rules ... She should also consider this, that there is no means of atoning for this sin; no way she can approach the shrines or the altars of a pure woman, beloved of god ... ' (Thesleff 1965, 151-4=*WLGR* 107). Between the lines one can discern the practical reason why adultery could cause a serious problem in a society without sure contraception, and where citizenship (especially in Athens) is determined by the citizenship of one's parents. The 'law' about adultery implies that a wife by her chastity performed a valuable service to the state; in Athens a woman caught in adultery must not only be repudiated by her husband, but is forbidden to offer public sacrifice; a foreign woman and a prostitute is similarly excluded (we learn this from the case of the notorious Neaera's daughter Phano, who was both: Demosthenes 59.38=*WLGR* 76). Fifth- and fourth-century B.C. law forbids a woman to make a will or to own (at least in Athens) property other than her own clothes and jewellery, but the system also guarantees her financial protection and guardianship by her male relatives (Isaeus 10.10; Gould 1980, 50n.85).

That I have had to rely primarily on tragedy and comedy in the preceding discussion suggests yet another reason why we have so little detailed information about what non-mythical fifth- and fourth-century B.C. husbands and wives felt about each other. The only other sources of evidence, grave inscriptions, offer only very limited information. In the fifth century, epitaphs tend to emphasise the general archetypal forms of excellence: e.g. 'of a worthy wife this is the tomb here, by the road that throngs with people – of Aspasia, who is dead; in response to her noble disposition Euopides set up this monument for her; she was his consort' (139 Friedländer-Hoffleit=*WLGR* 23). In the fourth and third centuries, there is more emphasis on the relationship of individuals to their family (a pattern that is also represented in the arrangement of their tombs (Humphreys 1983, 104-18). The cause of death is mentioned, or some distinguishing feature; Melite was 'the best'; Dionysia 'did not admire clothes or gold when she was alive but her husband', who in return for her youth adorns her tomb (*IG* II²11162; cf. Euripides, *Alcestis* 288-9); Nicephorus left four children, 'and died in the arms of his good wife' (Kaibel 327=*IG* II²1094). But even these epitaphs are brief and general, and the sculptures that accompany them represent stereotypical scenes, with no attempt at realistic portraiture. We may learn more about the intensity of family affection from the consistency with which family members desire to be together: Aristotle's will ends with a request that the bones of his wife be exhumed and buried with his, 'in accordance with her own instructions' (Diogenes Laertius 5.16=*WLGR* 67).

We appear to have more specific information about 'real' people in the Hellenistic age and after because of an increasing emphasis on individuality in literature as well as in art. In a world greatly expanded by Alexander's conquests, it was less possible to define oneself as a member of a particular small community; a fifth- or fourth-century epitaph might speak of a woman's *hêlikia*, the group of contemporaries with whom she was educated in dance and song (e.g. Kaibel 73,78). Fourth-century epitaphs and inscriptions mention a woman's occupation, but particularly from the point of view of the bereaved: 'Phanostrate, a midwife and physician lies here; she caused pain to none and all lamented her death' (Kaibel 45=Pleket 1); 'Hippostrate still misses you. "I loved you while you were alive, nurse, I love you still now even beneath the earth" ' (Kaibel 481=*IG* II²7873=*WLGR* 54). But in Greco-Roman Egypt and in Rome itself information is given on inscriptions that clearly distinguishes one person from another; a mother describes how she went from Athens to Alexandria when her daughter, one of Cleopatra's attendants, was sick, but arrived too late and brought her remains back to Athens (Kaibel 118=*WLGR* 62).

As concerns women's relations to their husbands, one gets the impression that in Hellenistic Egypt women were freer to move about, and were no longer closely restricted to the house by custom. In Theocritus' *Idyll* 15, set in suburban Alexandria, a woman calls on a woman friend and they go together to the festival of Adonis; but their conversation tells us that their husbands still do the shopping and make the decisions about where they are to live; the wife can complain, but cannot change the decision. A woman was able to make a will in her own name, and could decide how to dispose of the property she inherited from her father, but as in fifth- and fourth-century B.C. Athens, the document must be approved by a male guardian (*SB* X.10756=*WLGR* 202; Pomeroy 1985, 89-90). Legal documents protect the status of both wives and concubines, in the case of divorce or transfer, or rate of payment of a dowry (Pomeroy 1981, 308-9); perhaps such contracts always existed, at least verbally, but we know about them only from Egypt, because the climate was able to preserve them. Roman law, particularly in the Empire, spells out the rights of women in detail, drawing many subtle distinctions and allowing for exceptions with a precision and flexibility that was not possible in Classical Athens, where individual cases were subsumed into the general *nomos*. Roman law thus gives the impression that there was a considerable improvement (from our point of view) in women's status. But in practice, notions of the proper role of wives do not seem to have undergone any radical change.

In the Roman Empire, epitaphs in Greek, perhaps because of the conventions established in Classical models, continue to emphasise the standard qualities: chastity, care for husband and children, management of household (*oikos*); for example, this second-century A.D. inscription from Pergamum:

Farewell, lady Panthia from your husband. After your departure, I keep up my lasting grief for your cruel death. Hera, goddess of marriage, never saw such a wife: your beauty, your wisdom, your chastity. You bore me children completely like myself; you cared for your bridegroom and your children; you guided straight the rudder of life in our home and raised high our common fame in healing – though you were a woman you were not behind me in skill. In recognition of this your bridegroom Glycon built this tomb for you. I also buried here the body of (my father) immortal Philadelphus, and I myself will lie here when I die, since with you alone I shared my bed when I was alive, so may I cover myself in ground that we share. (Pleket 20=*WLGR* 125).

Again, as in fourth-century B.C. Athens, though now it is stated explicitly, the pattern of burial represents the unity of the family in life. Custom now permits a fuller description of the *oikos*; it is sustained not by farming, like most *oikoi* in Attica, but by the practice of healing, in which both husband and wife share. The statement 'Though you were a woman you were not behind me in skill' sounds condescending, but (like so many condescending remarks) was meant as a compliment; like Admetus, Glycon assumes his own priority, both as the head of the household and as a man.

Latin inscriptions, especially from the Empire, provide even more detail; some record whole eulogies which, like Roman portraits, lead us to believe that we might be able literally to recognise the people they describe: specific incidents from the past are mentioned, appearances are described, conversations remembered. We learn why a person has claim to the standard virtues ascribed to him or to her. One of the most famous of these long inscriptions is the eulogy by a husband for a woman who is not named but has been traditionally identified with the heroic Turia (*ILS* 8393=*WLGR* 207; Wistrand 1976; Gordon 1977, 7-12; Horsfall 1983; Mazzolani 1982). The husband records how his wife helped avenge her parents' deaths, after they were murdered during the civil war (1.3ff.); how she raised some young female relatives and gave them dowries from her own inheritance (1.4ff.); how she helped bring her husband back safely from exile during the proscriptions in 42 B.C. (2.2aff.), when the triumvir Marcus Lepidus objected to her husband's return: 'When you prostrated yourself at (Lepidus') feet, he not only did *not* raise you up, but dragged you along and abused you as though a common slave; your body was all covered with bruises, yet with unflinching steadfastness of purpose, you recalled to him Caesar's [i.e. Octavian's] edict of pardon and the letter of felicitation on my return that accompanied it. Braving his taunts and suffering the most brutal treatment, you denounced these cruelties publicly so that Lepidus was branded as the author of all my perils and misfortunes' (2.14-18). The husband even claims that her protest was instrumental in bringing about Lepidus' downfall (2.19ff.). This wife's performance was not unique: the historian Appian recalls other cases of wives interceding for their husbands, or determining, despite great hardship, to go into exile with them. Wartime conditions demanded that women go to extremes to preserve the unity of their families (Appian 4.39-40).

But Turia's sacrifices for her husband were not limited to wartime. Her husband explains that when they found that they were unable to have children, 'You did not believe you could be fertile and were disconsolate to see me without children; you did not wish me by continuing my marriage to you to give up hope of having children, and to be on that account unhappy, so you proposed divorce, that you would vacate the house and turn it over to a woman more fertile; your only intention was that because of our mutual affection (*concordia*) you yourself would search for and provide me with a worthy spouse, and that you would affirm that you would have treated the children as your own; and you said that you would make no division between inheritances which we had heretofore held in common, but that it would continue to be left in my control, or if I wished in your management; nothing would be sequestered, and you would have nothing separate, and that you would henceforth render to me

the services and devotion of a sister or mother-in-law' (2.31-9).
Most interestingly for us, the husband records his response to
this extraordinary offer, and it is not at all what one would
expect him to say from a Marxist or a feminist point of view: 'I
will admit that I was so irritated and shocked by such a
proposition that I had difficulty in restraining my anger and in
remaining master of myself. You spoke of divorce before the
decree of fate had forced us to separate, and I could not
comprehend how you could conceive of any reason why you,
while I was still alive, should not be my wife, you who while I was
in exile virtually from life had always remained most faithful'
(2.40-3). 'How could my desire to or need for having children
have been so great, that for that reason I would have broken my
promise to you, and exchanged what I could count on for
uncertainties? There is nothing more to say. You remained in my
house; I could not have agreed to your request without disgracing
myself or causing us both unhappiness' (2.44-7). The husband
concludes that the oration by stating: 'You deserved all, and I
must remain without having been able to give you all; your
wishes have been my law, and I will continue to provide whatever
still has been permitted for me to do' (2.67-8). This wife's
self-sacrifice and deference to her husband apparently not only
set an example for Octavian, but for the husband himself; even
though Octavian once he became emperor offered prizes for the
begetting of children (Dio Cassius 54.10). The husband refused
to accept his wife's offer of divorce and remained childless,
rather than lose her. So Andromache may not have been
overstating her case when she claimed that by extraordinary
service (in her case nursing her husband's bastards) she 'won her
husband over' by her excellence (Euripides, *Andromache* 207-8).

The 'Turia' inscription indicates that in certain upper-class
Roman marriages, wives could and did participate in all
important decisions, as one would expect, because the law
allowed them to own property, did not deny them access to the
outside world and specified their rights (Ciccotti 1985, 8). But
technically a woman may have been freer to determine the
course of her own life than most chose to be in practice. A woman
like the notorious Clodia, who entertained a sequence of
boyfriends, including perhaps Catullus, in her house after her
husband's death, was fair game for a lawyer like Cicero, who
could effectively destroy her credibility simply by contrasting

her life-style with approved patterns of behaviour (Lefkowitz 1981, 32-40). The highest compliment on epitaphs remained service to home and husband; in another eulogy, composed about the same time, a son praises his mother Murdia for being 'on an equal level with other good women in modesty, propriety, chastity, obedience, woolworking, and industry' (*ILS* 8394=*WLGR* 139; Horsfall 1982), as well as for her sound financial judgment and generosity to her children by two marriages.

Turia's husband relates that he 'had difficulty in restraining his anger and remaining master' of himself, but that was only in response to his wife's extraordinary generosity. There is a consistent emphasis even in shorter grave inscriptions in this period and after on domestic harmony: for example, 'For Lollia Victoriana his sweetest wife Lollianus Porresimus the Procurator bought this monument, because she deserved it. With her he lived twenty years without any fault-finding on either side. That is having loved' (*CIL* 10.1951). In an inscription from Carthage, a wife says she 'set up this monument to her blessed husband, who was most generous and dutiful; while I lived with him, he never said a cruel word to me, never gave offence to me or any one else' (Lattimore 1962, 277-80). It would be naive to take these or any eulogies or epitaphs as precise representations of the truth, but at least they offer valid testimony to an ideal. These wives, like the fourth-century B.C. Athenian woman who wanted to remain with her bankrupt husband, appreciated their husband's constant 'affection'.

One expects to find lower-class wives to be involved in their husbands' occupation; we find pairs of grocers in both Greek and Latin inscriptions. In first-century B.C. Rome a butcher in praising his wife includes financial honesty among the list of traditional virtues. 'She lived as a faithful wife to a faithful husband with affection equal to my own, since she never let avarice keep her from her duty' (*ILS* 7472). His wife, on the same inscription, claims that her husband 'flourished at all times through her diligent performance of duty'. But the 'Turia' inscription and many of the anecdotes about wives' heroism in times of persecution, suggest that political circumstances could encourage close companionship also among upper-class couples. As a final example, I would like to consider a long inscription about a husband and wife in the late fourth century A.D.; their account of their lives is of particular interest because the husband, Praetextatus, was one of the last important pagans, who held office not only under Julian the Apostate but under several Christian emperors (Bloch 1963, 193-218). What he and his wife Paulina are represented as saying about each other is virtually the last evidence we have of pagan ideals.

The grave monument (*ILS* 4154=*WLGR* 264a) of Praetextatus and Paulina is inscribed on all four sides; the front lists their names and their religious offices, and some of Praetextatus' public offices (Bloch 1945, 199-244). On the sides of the monument are eulogies in verse to Paulina: on the right side she is said to be 'conscious of truth and chastity, devoted to temples and friend of the divinities: she put her husband before herself, and Rome before her husband, proper, faithful, pure in mind and body, kindly to all, helpful to her family gods'; in earlier inscriptions, a wife or husband's piety might be routinely mentioned (Alcestis before her death prayed to Hestia and decorated all the altars), but here it is explicitly detailed, and there is a striking emphasis on her patriotism. The inscription on the right side of the monument speaks of her devotion to husband and family, but also of 'the experience of our life together, the alliance of our marriage, our pure, faithful, simple concord; you helped your husband, loved him, honoured him, cared for him.'

On the back of the monument Paulina gives (again in verse) an even more detailed eulogy of Praetextatus. She claims that her greatest honour is having been his wife; she praises him for his civic achievement and for his scholarship. But she places even more importance on his religious piety: 'You as pious initiate conceal in the secrecy of your mind what was revealed in the sacred mysteries, and you with knowledge worship the manifold divinity of the gods; you kindly include as colleague in the rites your wife, who is respectful of men and gods and is faithful to you ... My husband, by the gift of your learning you keep me from the fate of death pure and chaste; you take me into the temples and devote me as the servant of the gods. With you as my witness I am introduced to all the mysteries; you, my pious consort, honour me as priestess of Dindymene and Attis with the sacrificial rites of the taurobolium; you instruct me as minister of Hecate in the triple secret and you make me worthy of the rites of the Greek Ceres ... Now men, now women approve the insignia that you as teacher have given me.' From this inscription and other evidence we have about Praetextatus, it seems that for him religion was closely bound up with his service to the state; apparently when he was governor of Achaea in A.D. 362 under Julian he restored some of the cults that he and his wife were initiated into. Her eulogy of him indicates that he served both as her mentor and teacher; but it is significant that he wanted her to share in the rituals he himself took so seriously. I am inclined to think she meant what she said about her gratitude for having been included in this important aspect of his life, first because the monument was put up after his death (whoever composed the elegant verse), and secondly because other aristocratic women are eager to record their participation in some of the same rituals. It seems that members of family groups would be initiated together, especially in rituals like the taurobolium (e.g. *ILS* 4154); so perhaps a pagan husband's taking a close interest in his wife's religious education is not as unusual as evidence gleaned from the Christian Fathers might suggest (cf. Brown 1972, 172-3).

If in this chapter I have sought to show that certain attitudes persisted throughout classical antiquity, despite significant changes in women's legal status and over a great range of time as well as geography, I am not trying to argue that all ancient marriages were happy, or that in contemporary society we should accept ancient values. After all, so far as we know, every document we have considered was written or at least inscribed (since only men were stone-cutters) by a man, and some men may only have been able to hear part of what the women were saying to them. In his treatise *Advice on Marriage*, Plutarch urges the bridegroom to be understanding and faithful; but it is clear from what he says that he expected most of the adjustments to be made by the wife: he advocates the kind of marriage described in the inscription about Praetextatus and Paulina; the woman should worship the husband's gods; marriage should be a partnership; a wife ought to be able to say, 'Dear husband, to me you are guide, philosopher and teacher in all that is beautiful and most divine'; women should study geometry and philosophy to put their mind on higher things (*Moralia* 145c-d). He believes that woman can and should be educated, though as tradition would dictate within the context of their husbands' homes. Clearly he means his advice for the best;

can we really blame him for not being able to imagine a system in which women could be completely independent? He was an antiquarian and historian and he had studied and read enough to know that the concept of a married woman's role had not changed very much over seven hundred years.

5

Influential Women

When Greek colonists set up new cities in the then unknown frontier of Italy, they were quick to find myths that connected them with their ancestors, and that gave their customs and their shrines legitimacy. So it should be no surprise that people who initiate new styles of government or patterns of living – political colonists, we might call them – also seek precedents in the prestigious civilisations of the past. Proponents of slavery in the United States discovered Greek and Roman writings that supported their views; so, of course, did the Abolitionists (Wiesen 1976, 199-212). Karl Marx found that the notion of free, rather than enforced, sale of labour first occurred in the Roman army (de Ste. Croix 1981, 24-5). Feminists, in addition to producing evidence for matriarchal societies, have called attention to the extraordinary achievements of a few women, as if they set a pattern that twentieth-century women might emulate and revive, and finally bring into full realisation.

When I observe that in the ancient world women neither had nor sought political power for themselves, but worked through their husbands or fathers or sons, people often object: what about Antigone, Clytemnestra, Artemisia, Agrippina? But I believe that it is possible to show in all these cases, as well as in many others, that women take political action only under certain closely defined conditions, and that unless they do so at least ostensibly on behalf of a male relative they and others around them come to a bad end. I will begin by talking about women in myth, that is, in specific works of literature, because myths illustrate common attitudes more clearly and simply than history; but history too can be shown to follow the patterns of myth, in part because those were the only terms in which most writers could interpret human experience, and in part because ancient societies for practical reasons offered women little opportunity to act as individuals outside the context of their families.

Ancient women could certainly be courageous, but they could not be truly independent. Antigone herself is an example. In Sophocles' drama, she contrives to bury her brother in defiance of an order by her uncle Creon, the king of Thebes, that her brother Polynices, who had attacked his homeland, should remain unburied. Denial of burial was a traditional penalty for treason; but Antigone has the moral sensibility to see that Creon's order runs counter to another established custom, the obligation of the family or *genos* to bury and to worship the remains of their deceased members (Lacey 1968, 54-5, 80-1).

Recently feminist critics have suggested that Antigone, in taking action against her sister's advice and Creon's edict, assumes an essentially masculine role (Foley 1975, 36; Sorum 1982, 206; O'Brien 1977, xiii-xxx); that in defending her blood relationship to Polynices, she 'must undercut the form and potential of the family' (Sorum 1982, 207); that Antigone has adopted the aggressive stance of an Orestes, 'a younger son revenging or redeeming the death of an unburied brother' (Heilbrun 1973, 9). In the process of interpretation these critics assume that Creon, or the city elders in the chorus, represent not themselves but the State, a government supported and accepted by the majority of Theban citizens, whose laws and customs Antigone is threatening (Foley 1975, 33-6); therefore, the drama *Antigone* calls into question the traditional structure of society.

But I do not believe that Sophocles or his audience would have seen Antigone's action as unconventional, or have recognised in the play an attempt to define or promote new family structures or modes of behaviour. In the first place, it is not established custom that Antigone opposes, but the orders of one particular individual, Creon; Creon himself may equate his own opinions with the city's (e.g. 736), but the outcome of the drama makes it clear that he is mistaken. The analogy of Antigone to Orestes is misleading, because Antigone is not trying to avenge or redeem her brother's death, but is seeking only to bury him with appropriate rites for the dead. The difference may seem trivial to us, but to the Greeks it was (and in remote villages still is) essential; men avenge murders of kin, women prepare bodies for burial and sing laments over the body (Campbell 1964, 193-4, 168-9; Alexiou 1974, 22).

If Sophocles from time to time in the play states explicitly that Antigone and her sister Ismene are women, it is to emphasise to his audience that Creon's edict violates established custom, and that by demanding obedience to it he is misusing his power as a ruler, that is, he is behaving like a tyrant. 'Consider,' says Ismene to Antigone at the beginning of the drama, 'that we two are left alone [i.e. without father or brothers to protect them], and how cruelly we will perish, if we oppose the edict of the king (*turannon*) or his power. You must remember that the two of us are born women and as such do not fight with men; since we are in the power of those who are stronger, we must obey these orders, and orders even more painful than these' (61-4). When he has Creon complain that he would be weaker than a woman if he allowed her to get away with disobeying his order (525, 579), or insist that 'she and her sister must now be women and not allowed outside the house' (579), Sophocles is not describing normal male-female relations; he is portraying a man desperately trying to justify a decision that only he in the whole city (690ff.) considers to be correct.

In fact, far from being unconventional, Antigone is only doing what her family might have expected of her, as she herself says: 'But I have great hope that when I come [to the lower world] I shall come welcome to my father, and welcome to you, mother, and welcome to you, dear brother, since when each of you died I washed and dressed you and poured libations on your tombs' (897-902). In the fifth and fourth centuries B.C. (i.e. in Sophocles' lifetime and for a century afterwards), it was common belief that families were reunited in death (Humphreys 1983, 106; Lacey 1968, 148-9). Special care was taken to bury family members in the same plot, even if bones had to be exhumed from other localities and re-buried. I do not think an ancient audience would have considered it unusual or excessive when Sophocles' Electra laments over what she supposes to be the urn that holds her brother's ashes: 'So now you receive me into this house of yours, I who am nothing to your nothing, so that for the rest of time I can live with you below; for when we were above ground I shared the same things with you, and now I wish to die and not be left outside your tomb' (*Electra* 1165-9). When Antigone is captured, even Ismene asks to die with her and to give the rites to their dead brother (544-5). The guard who catches Antigone says that when she saw the corpse of Polynices unburied, 'she wailed out the sharp cry of an anguished bird, as when in its empty nest it sees its bed stripped of its nestlings' (424-5). To us Antigone's or Electra's failure to distinguish between living and dead may seem strange; but to Antigone the important link was not life but blood-kinship: 'My life died long ago, so that I might serve my dead [family]' (559-60). Antigone says explicitly that she would not have risked her life for a husband, or if she had had children of her own; but without any other family, her first duty was to her brother – whether dead or alive does not seem to matter. Nor does Ismene count as a reason for her to stay alive, because she is female, and so not able to inherit or continue the family line. When Antigone replies to Creon's accusations that she could disobey his edict, but not the 'unwritten customs' (*agrapta nomima*) of the gods, she is simply claiming that family loyalty must take precedence over rulings that have not existed since time immemorial; she is not questioning Creon's right to power or the structure of government, but his own intelligence and judgment: 'If I had put up with [?] my mother's son having died an unburied corpse, that would have caused me pain; but I am not pained by what I have done. If I seem to you to have acted foolishly, then I have been accused of folly by a fool' (466-70).

To put it another way, Antigone must be female for the dramatic action to occur in the first place, because only a mother or sister would have felt so strongly the obligation to bury the dead (Daube 1972, 6-7). As Ismene suggests, it would have been possible for her instead to ask the gods of the lower world for forgiveness, if she had failed to bury her brother, on the ground that she was forcibly prevented by the rulers of Thebes (66-7). It would also have been possible for her to have tried first to work through a man, like Haemon; as Aethra persuaded her son Theseus to allow the mothers of the Argive heroes who fell at Thebes to bury their sons. 'It's natural for women, if they are clever, to do everything through men' (Euripides, *Suppliant Women* 40-1). We might choose to call her courageous or generous, but the chorus states that she is foolish: 'Unhappy child of an unhappy father Oedipus; what has happened? It isn't true that they have caught you in folly and bring you in disobedient to the king's laws?' (379-82). They regard her, as she does herself, as a victim of the family curse that destroyed her

parents and her brother: 'Your respect [for your brother] is one
kind of right respect, but one also ought not to transgress in any
way the power of him to whom power belongs. Your self-willed
anger has destroyed you' (872-5). This anger and folly
(*aphrosunê*, 'un-thinking') are aspects of the family curse, and
the action of the curse, far from being disapproved of by the gods,
is part of their system: 'Evil seems good to the person whose
mind the god is leading toward delusion' (622-3).

I would not have been able to see several years ago, and in a
way regret that I must now admit, that Sophocles' audience
would have seen Antigone's action as courageous, laudable, but
risky (she does end up dead, after all), and certainly within the
bounds of acceptable female behaviour. Antigone's conduct does
not set a new revolutionary standard any more than it can be
said to serve as a prototype of female Christian martyrdom – an
interpretation that profoundly impressed the composer Mendelssohn, even though he knew no Greek (Jacob 1963, 290; Jebb 1900,
xlii). Like other women in epic and drama, Antigone wins praise
for acting on behalf of her family: Penelope deceives the suitors
(and so holds out for her husband Odysseus) for three years
before she is discovered unravelling her weaving at night;
Andromache defies Hermione and Menelaus in order to protect
her young son; Iphigenia tricks the wicked king in order to save
her brother Orestes; Helen tells lies to rescue Menelaus. It is
important to note that in all these cases the women offer only
passive resistance. Apparently acts of treachery are acceptable
in a woman only if they are non-violent and are undertaken on
behalf of a male relative.

But a woman is not permitted, even with justification, to take
the law into her own hands. After the fall of Troy, when all the
Trojan men are dead, Hecuba herself avenges the murder of her
youngest son Polydorus. He had been sent to Polymestor in
Thrace for safekeeping, but Hecuba discovers that Polymestor
has murdered him, and when Polymestor arrives in Troy with his
young sons in the hope of collecting more money, Hecuba and
her servant women use their brooches to put out Polymestor's
eyes and to stab his sons to death. Polymestor asks Agamemnon
to punish Hecuba, but Agamemnon lets her get away with her
revenge. 'Alas,' Polymestor complains, 'it seems that I have been
defeated by a woman and a slave, and suffer vengeance from my
inferiors' (Euripides, *Hecuba* 1252-3). But Hecuba's triumph is

short-lived: Polymestor predicts that Hecuba will throw herself from the ship that takes her from Troy and be turned into a dog, and that her grave will be known as the 'poor dog's tomb', a landmark for sailors (1273). Her death, in other words, will be sordid (the Greeks did not like dogs), and more significantly, anonymous. On the other hand, for Penelope, who could leave the execution of the suitors to her husband and son, 'for her the fame of her virtue (aretê) will never perish; the immortals will fashion a lovely song for mortal men about good Penelope; she did not devise evil deeds, like Tyndareus' daughter [Clytemnestra], killing her wedded husband; but for Clytemnestra there will be a hateful song among men, and she will give women a bad reputation, even to the woman who does good deeds' (Odyssey 24.196-202).

It may seem unfair that the speaker of these lines, the dead Agamemnon, believes that no woman can be trusted after what Clytemnestra did. Polymestor, too, after he has described to Agamemnon how the Trojan women stabbed his children and put his own eyes out, concludes by condemning women in general: 'Neither sea nor land sustains a race like them' (1181-2), in other words, they are monsters (cf. Aeschylus, Libation Bearers 585ff.). Semonides of Amorgos, in his satire on women (fr.7W=WLGR 30), identifies, as we have seen, nine types of bad women, but only one good type. Perhaps the low proportion of good women could be taken as evidence of enduring misogyny on the part of (male) Greek poets; but it is important to remember that these statements about bad women all occur in the context of invective, and so are likely to be exaggerated. Compare how an angry woman who feels she has been wronged, like Medea in Euripides' drama, contrasts the unfortunate lot of (all) women with the enviable life led – without exception – by men (230ff.).

It is also possible to argue that the limitations that apply to women in epic and in drama apply as well to the 'political' women in Aristophanes' comedies. Lysistrata in particular is often cited as the first liberated woman; but consider what she actually accomplishes. In order to bring about peace, she summons all Greek women to a meeting (they of course arrive late), and gets them to swear not to have sexual intercourse with their husbands until the men agree to end the war between Athens and Sparta. Her plan works, and then her organisation of women disbands and the women go back to their husbands. So, even in the fantasy world of comedy, women only take action to preserve and to return to their families. Women have intelligence and understanding, but speak out only in emergencies, and even then their models are men. Lysistrata says, as she concludes the peace, 'Although I am a woman, I have intelligence [quoting from a lost play, Euripides' *Melanippe the Wise*]; for my own part, I do not have bad judgment. I have listened to many speeches by my father and older men and so am not badly educated' (*Lysistrata* 1125-7). When in the *Thesmophoriazusae* the women meet to attack Euripides, their proceedings are a burlesque of the Athenian men's assembly. Aristophanes realises that his audience would find the very notion of women meeting together, making speeches and voting, hilariously funny.

In the comedy *Ecclesiazusae* (or 'Women Meeting in the Assembly') women in male disguise manage to infiltrate the assembly and vote to let women run the city, on the grounds that 'we [the assembly] ought to turn the city over to women, for we use them also as guardians and stewards in our households' (210-12). The infiltrated assembly passes two new laws: (1) that all possessions (including wives and children) shall be held in ccmmon, and (2) that the ugliest and oldest women will have first chance at getting men. The first law is a parody of what Athenians understood to be the constitution of Sparta; after Athens lost the war to Sparta, the Spartan system of government appeared to have special merit. In 392 B.C., when the *Ecclesiazusae* was performed, Aristophanes still could make fun of the notion that women might have equal rights with men. A generation later Plato realised that people might still ridicule the idea that women should be educated (*Republic* 452b), but none the less he incorporated into the model government of his Republic equal education for men and women and common marriages and children, so that women might be able to be companions of men and co-guardians of his ideal state (456b). But even in his utopia Plato included the proviso that women, because their natures were weaker, should be assigned lighter duties in wartime (he does not specify what they would be).

Of course such socialistic theories, however much they were debated in intellectual circles, were never practised, at least in Athens (Annas 1981, 181-5; cf. Adam 1963, I 345). In fact, Aristotle claimed that the liberty permitted to Spartan women in the days of Sparta's great military successes had by the middle of the fourth century B.C. led directly to her defeat by the Thebans. Women, he observed, had not been subject to the same restrictions as men under the Spartan constitution, and so lived intemperate and luxurious lives, while the men remained in military training. As a result, the Spartan women at the time of the Theban invasion of 369 were 'utterly useless and caused more confusion than the enemy' (*Politics* 1269b5). 'The disorder of women,' he observed, 'not only of itself gives an air of indecorum to the state, but tends to foster avarice' (1207a9). In his view, one particularly unfortunate consequence was that two-fifths of Sparta was owned by women (1270a10-11), who unlike their Athenian counterparts could inherit and bequeath property (Cartledge 1981, 86-9).

Here, as in his theories of human physiology, Aristotle appears to regard as normative what was acceptable in Athenian life and to consider all other practices deviations. But he and not Plato had the last word. If Greek women – in history or in literature – ever had an opportunity to govern, it was only for a brief period, in order to cope with a particular problem or emergency, or in the case of monarchies and tyrannies, if they happened (like Artemisia or Cynna) to be related to the man in charge.

I will now consider briefly the role played by women in history, as opposed to women in literature, to the extent that the two can be separated. References to women by biographers and historians tend to be anecdotal, and so not necessarily pinned down to particular times or events; rather, they are illustrative of character in general and timeless ways. For example, Cornelia is praised by several ancient writers for having educated her sons the Gracchi, but how and when and what she taught them is not specified. But whatever the source of the information, the same rules seem to apply in history as well as in myth: women can affect the course of political events only if they act through or on behalf of the men in their families. They can take independent action, like Lysistrata, in an emergency, but then must retire when the problem is solved. The earliest instance of such an event in history is recorded by Plutarch in his treatise on the bravery of women. Early in the fifth century B.C., according to Plutarch, Telesilla of Argos, an aristocrat who because of her weak constitution had been encouraged to compose poetry, when the Argive army had suffered a severe setback, organised the women of Argos to arm themselves and successfully defend their city's fortifications against the Spartans (*Moralia* 245c-f). But as soon as the crisis was over the women resumed their conventional roles; according to Herodotus (who does not mention Telesilla) the Argive women were married to slaves (6.83.1), or as Plutarch insists, because they deserved better, to the aristocratic citizens of the neighbouring cities.

Plutarch also preserves another dramatic instance of a woman's political effectiveness in a crisis, this time, as he says from a period much closer to his own time, the first century B.C. (Stadter 1965, 101-3). Aretaphila of Cyrene was compelled to marry the tyrant who had murdered her husband. First she tried to poison him. She survived torture when her plot failed, and succeeded in getting rid of her tyrant husband by marrying her daughter to his brother and persuading him to murder his brother. Finally she contrived to have the ruler of a neighbouring state capture her son-in-law and turn him and his mother over to the citizens of Cyrene to be murdered. The people of Cyrene treated her like a hero, and asked her to share in the government and management of the city with the aristocrats, but she 'as if she had played in a sort of drama or competed in a contest up to the point of winning the prize', returned home to the women's quarters and spent the rest of her life working at her loom in the company of her family (*Moralia* 257d-e).

Even if the original story of Aretaphila has been embellished by Plutarch or his sources to the point where it conforms with the standard pattern of women's behaviour in myth, it does indicate how implausible it seemed even in the Hellenistic age that women should share in the actual process of government (*sunarchein, sundioikein*, 257d). It seems clear from papyri and inscriptions – the most authentic contemporary evidence preserved about the role of women in public life – that even when women were legally entitled to own property and to make wills they were welcomed as benefactors of cities and given honorific titles, but never a real place on the town council or an actual vote in the assembly. The traditional female virtues were listed along with their benefactions, and even though their own names are now conspicuously mentioned (unlike proper aristocratic women in the fifth and fourth centuries B.C., who remained incognito (Schaps 1977, 323-30), due credit was always given to the *men* in their families: 'Phile, daughter of Apollonius, wife of Thessalus son of Polydeuces; as the first woman *stephanephorus*, she

dedicated at her own expense a receptacle for water and the
water pipes in the city [Priene]' (Pleket 5=*WLGR* 48, 1st cent.
B.C.); 'The council and the people, to Flavia Publicia
Nicomachis, daughter of Dinomachus and Procle ... their
benefactor, and benefactor through her ancestors, founder of our
city, president for life, in recognition of her complete virtue'
(Pleket 19=*WLGR* 162, Asia Minor, 2nd cent. A.D.); Aurelia
Leite, 'daughter of Theodotus, wife of the foremost man in the
city, Marcus Aurelius Faustus ... she was gymnasiarch of the
gymnasium which she repaired and renewed when it had been
dilapidated for many years ... She loved wisdom, her husband,
her children, her native city [Paros]' (Pleket 31=*WLGR* 164, 300
A.D.).

Philosophical theory, as so often, was based on and reinforced
social practice. Aristotle believed that women were capable of
virtue and of understanding, though he could not accept what
Plato proposed, that self-control, courage and justice were the
same for women and for men. Aristotle stated that 'men's
courage is shown in commanding (or ruling, *archein*) and
women's in obeying' (*Politics* 1260a8). A treatise on women
written in the third or second century B.C. by Neopythagorean
philosophers in Italy, in the form of a letter from one woman to
another, also assumes that a woman's capacity to govern was
considerably less than a man's: 'Some people think that it is not
appropriate for a woman to be a philosopher, just as a woman
should not be a cavalry officer or a politician ... I agree that men
should be generals and city officials and politicians, and women
should keep house and stay inside and receive and take care of
their husbands. But I believe that courage, justice and
intelligence are qualities that men and women have in common
... Courage and intelligence are more appropriately male
qualities because of the strength of men's bodies and the power
of their minds. Chastity is more appropriately female' (Thesleff
1965, 151).

The apparent exceptions only prove the rule that women could
not be accepted as governors unless they acted in conjunction
with a man. Hellenistic queens have been regarded as the first
examples of truly independent women (Pomeroy 1985, 17-30).
They organised court intrigues (including murders); they
directed strategy of naval and land battles; they made decisions
affecting governmental policy. But it is important to remember

that even the most capable of these women worked through or at least with the titular presence of a male consort (Cantarella 1981, 113-14). Arsinoe, queen of Egypt from 274 to 270 B.C., enjoyed power as the consort of her brother; Berenice, wife and cousin of Arsinoe's adopted son Ptolemy III Euergetes, was praised by Callimachus for the courage she showed as a young girl, which won her her husband (Macurdy 1932, 130-6). The unwritten law appears to be that the co-ruling (*sunarchein*) and co-management (*sundioikein*) unthinkable for Aretaphila in conjunction with unrelated males (above, p.88), is available to women with husbands, fathers or brothers. Cleopatra VII came to the throne with her brother. Then she enlisted the aid first of Julius Caesar, who became at least for a short time her consort, to remain on the throne by defeating her brother and installing a younger brother as co-ruler. Then she used Mark Antony to stay in power, though even when she sat with Antony on twin thrones she was addressed as 'co-ruler with Caesarion', her son (allegedly) by Caesar (Plutarch, *Antony* 54; cf. Pomeroy 1985, 24-8; Macurdy 1932, 202-5). For ordinary women also civil law ensured that men had at least nominal control. Greek women in the Hellenistic age could draw up contracts and make wills, but only with the consent of a male guardian or *kurios*, usually a close relative (Pomeroy 1985, 119-20).

Upper-class Romans in Cicero's day could claim that their wives enjoyed greater social freedom than women in Greek cities (Nepos, *praef.* 6); the aristocratic Aretaphila of Greek Cyrene returned to the women's quarters and saw only other women and members of her family. But, as we have seen (p.74), inscriptions and letters explain how Roman women assisted the men in their families in their political careers. Turia's husband records how his wife managed to have him brought back from exile, and indicates how her accusations helped contribute to the triumvir Lepidus' downfall (cf. Balsdon 1962, 204-5). The proscriptions of the triumvirs apparently elicited similarly heroic behaviour on the part of other aristocrats' wives (Ciccotti 1985, 24-6): Acilius' wife (like a proper Athenian woman, her own name is not given) bribed soldiers with her jewellery not to turn her husband over to be executed; Lentulus' wife donned male disguise in order to join her husband in exile; Rheginus' wife hid her husband in a sewer; Coponius' wife slept with Antony in order to purchase her husband's safety, 'thus curing one evil with another', as the historian Appian remarks (*Civil Wars* 4.39-40=*WLGR* 208).

Brutus, the murderer of Caesar, appears to have been aided at every step in his career by his mother Servilia (Balsdon 1962, 51). Certainly one reason why Caesar pardoned Brutus after he had fought against him in 48 B.C. was that Servilia had been his mistress. After the conspiracy that led to Caesar's death, she received and transmitted messages for her son (*ad Att.* 416.4). Cicero in a letter describes how she took charge of a family conference at Antium at which she contrived to silence even Cicero with the comment that she had 'never heard anything like' what he was proposing; she herself proposed to have legislation changed on her son's behalf, and apparently was successful (389.2). But for all her initiative, Cicero himself clearly thinks of her as her son's agent, rather than as an independent operator. He remarks to his friend Atticus (whom he teased about having Servilia as a 'pal', *familiaris*, 389.2): 'It's just like you not to fault Servilia, which is to say, Brutus' (394).

Women in Pompeii joined with men in supporting candidates for local political offices, as graffiti on painted walls reveal: 'Amadio along with his wife asks you to vote for Gnaeus Sabinus for aedile' (*CIL* iv. 913=*WLGR* 210). Some of the men and women appear to have been co-workers in shops: 'Appuleia and Narcissus along with their neighbour Mustius, ask you to vote for Pupius' (*ILS* 6408a). One woman, Statia, asks on her own for support of her candidate (*CIL* iv.3684) – she, of course, could not vote for him herself.

But generally women who spoke out on their own behalf, rather than on behalf of a close male relative, were criticised for being selfish, licentious and avaricious. The speech attributed by Livy to the formidable moralist Cato the Elder provides an example of the kind of thing that was said about ambitious women; the issue is whether to repeal the Oppian law limiting women's right to own property (195 B.C.): 'Our ancestors did not want women to conduct any – not even private – business without a guardian; they wanted them to be under the authority of parents, brothers, or husbands; we (the gods help us!) even now let them snatch at the government and meddle in the Forum and our assemblies ... Give rein to their unbridled natures and these unmastered creatures, and hope that they will put limits on their own freedom! They want freedom, nay licence (if we are to speak the truth) in all things ... If they are victorious now, what will they not attempt? As soon as they begin to be your equals, they will have become your superiors ... ' (34.2.11-3.2). Of Sempronia, who supported the conspiracy of Catiline (who was not a relative of hers), it was said, 'there was nothing she set a smaller value on than seemliness and chastity, and she was as careless of her reputation as she was of her money' (Sallust, *Catiline* 24-5=*WLGR* 203; Balsdon 1962, 47-8). We are told that one could use the name of Gaia Afrania (a contemporary of Caesar's) who brought lawsuits herself, without using (male) lawyers, to designate *any* woman with low morals (Valerius Maximus 8.3=*WLGR* 205).

In popular belief, not only was self-assertion on a woman's part regarded as self-indulgence and licentiousness; crowds of women were considered a public menace. Livy has Cato complain of the women seeking repeal of the Oppian law 'running around in public, blocking streets and speaking to other women's husbands'. In practice women were permitted to organise themselves into formal groups only for some social or religious purpose, rather on the lines of a modern ladies' auxiliary. For example, in the third century B.C. the matrons 'purely and chastely' dedicated a golden bowl to Juno out of contributions from their dowries (Livy 27.37.8-9=*WLGR* 238). Inscriptions from the Empire record grants of money donated to women's organisations for public services; and women apparently could meet to set rules of social conduct and to discipline one another (Suetonius, *Galba* 5.1; *Hist. Aug. Elag.* 4.3-4=*WLGR* 240).

On the other hand, Hortensia, herself daughter of a famous orator, was praised for pleading in 42 B.C. to the triumvirs that rich women be relieved of a special tax; 'Quintus Hortensius lived again in the female line and breathed in his daughter's words' (Val. Max. 8.3). Her speech – unlike that of any other woman – was said to have been preserved verbatim, probably because what she said would have won male approval. In the one version of the speech that has come down to us, she claims that women had never supported despotic governments in the past; she recalls to the triumvirs what women would have done to serve the state, and also reminds them that in the present crisis the women have lost fathers, husbands and sons. Significantly she does not dwell on issues like taxation without representation or women's rights, or the pleasures and luxuries that their money might buy (Appian, *Civil Wars* 4.32-3). If such arguments had

had any appeal, Livy would have put them into the mouth of
Valerius, the opponent of Cato the Elder in the senatorial debate
about the repeal of the Oppian law. But instead Livy makes
Valerius concentrate on the services that Roman women in the
past performed on behalf of their country. He allows Valerius
only one 'equal opportunity' argument, and this with great
condescension: men can wear the purple in civil magistracies not
available to women; depriving men of such honours 'could
wound the spirits of men; what do you think it could do to the
spirits of our little women (*mulierculae*), whom even small
problems disturb?' Livy's Valerius concludes by arguing that
women prefer that their adornment be subject to their husband's
or father's judgment rather than to a law: 'A woman's slavery is
never put off while her male relatives are safe and sound, and
they hate the liberty that widowhood or orphanage allows them
... It is for the weaker sex to submit to whatever you advise. The
more power you possess, all the more moderately you should
exercise your authority' (34.6-7).

Given this background, I do not find it at all surprising that
during the Empire, when the principal liberty guaranteed to
male citizens was the right to petition, that women's initiative
was restricted to helping male relatives (Millar 1977, 546-8).
Arria killed herself before her husband (who was about to be
taken away to be executed), while uttering the famous words,
'Look, it doesn't hurt' (Pliny, *Letters* 3.16=*WLGR* 150).
Agrippina, Nero's mother, was even more aggressive than
Servilia, Brutus' mother, in promoting her son's career. She
married her uncle, the emperor Claudius, and got him to appoint
her son as his heir.

Wives and mothers of emperors appeared on coins for
propaganda purposes, for example, Antony with Cleopatra
(Macurdy 1932, 205). Clearly the rulers of these vast and
constantly threatened realms needed the participation of wives
and mothers for political as well as for personal reasons (Balsdon
1962, 142, 160). Again mythology (i.e. literature) gives us the
best indication of the response the emperors were seeking to
elicit from their subjects. A man who had the support of a wife or
mother was more easily approachable and more capable of
clemency. In Euripides' drama *The Suppliant Woman*, the
mothers of the Argive captains who helped Polynices attack
Thebes first ask Aethra, Theseus' mother, not Theseus himself,

to help them get military protection so that they can bury their sons (Polynices' burial was not the only problem created by that war). The mothers appeal to Aethra: 'You have borne a son yourself, o queen' (55-6). When the king of Argos, Adrastus, fails to convince Theseus to help, Aethra intercedes. Theseus listens to her, because 'even women can provide much intelligent advice' (294). Aethra is successful where Antigone fails, because she is able to persuade Theseus to help; he is of course a much more reasonable man than Creon: 'For what will my detractors say, when you, my mother, who are anxious on my behalf, are the first to tell me to undertake this task [of allowing the Argive women to bury their dead]' (342-5).

In Rome, emperors' wives and even mistresses could save the lives (or fortunes) of individuals who were able to approach them directly and so get the emperor's ear. That, as we have seen, was only a traditional pattern of behaviour. But the pattern survived through the middle ages and well into our own time. By the fifth century A.D. the characterisation of Christian divinities had undergone subtle but important changes. In iconography Jesus, once kindly and approachable, had become more closely identified with and sometimes even indistinguishable from his father. To receive his mercy, appeal must be made to his mother, who in the synoptic gospels is not at all an important or influential figure (Warner 1976, 285-6). Thus the model of the 'power behind the throne' was incorporated into religion from the world of politics, and survives not only in modern Christianity, but in notions of approved behaviour for women in the twentieth century.

6

Martyrs

Of all the roles played by women in Greek myth certainly the most active, and therefore the most deserving of the praise ordinarily accorded to men, is self-sacrifice. Usually the occasion is presented by a battle: an oracle is given that in order to win a young person must be sacrificed to a god. The most famous incident is, of course, Agamemnon's sacrifice of his daughter Iphigenia, in a story told by Aeschylus in his drama *Agamemnon*. According to earlier accounts, the goddess allowed a deer to be substituted for the human child, a story that provided (among other things) an explanation of why the goddess accepted animal sacrifices before the battle (Henrichs 1981, 198-208). But by returning to what would have been considered a more primitive form of the myth, Aeschylus was able to emphasise the consequences of the taking of a human life, even when according to other ethical standards the killing might seem justified. Euripides also included myths of human sacrifice in several of his plays, and it is noteworthy that with one exception the victims are female. The preference in myth for the female sex is intriguing. It does not indicate that the Greeks considered female life less valuable – why then would the gods care to demand the sacrifice? – but rather, as the connection with the cult of the Mistress of Animals suggests, that women in religious terms were the most appropriate victims (Lloyd-Jones 1983, 89). But whatever the original significance in cult, female sacrifice in drama seems intended to demonstrate women's ability to be as courageous as men and as responsible for maintaining the values of society.

In the *Agamemnon* the sacrifice of Iphigenia is one (though not the only) justification offered by Clytemnestra for taking her husband's life; she blames the citizens of Argos for not having protested against his act:

Then you raised no opposition to this man who, holding it of no special account, as though it were the death of a beast, where sheep in their fleecy flocks abound, sacrificed his own child, a travail most dear to me, to charm the winds of Thrace. Was it not he whom you should have driven from this land, as penalty for his polluting act? (1413-20, tr. Lloyd-Jones 1982)

But the old men of Argos, though they took no action at the time, are not indifferent. In the account they give of the sacrifice in their opening song, they do not underestimate the difficulty of the decision, but they make it clear that Agamemnon did wrong in choosing to sacrifice his daughter:

And when he had put on the yoke-strap of compulsion, his spirit's wind veering to an impious blast, impure, unholy, from that moment his mind changed to a temper of utter ruthlessness. For mortals are made reckless by the evil counsels of merciless Infatuation (*parakopa*), beginner of disaster. And so he steeled himself to become the sacrificer of his daughter, to aid a war fought to avenge a woman's loss and to pay beforehand for his ships. (218-27)

It was, after all, possible for him not to pay the price, but to turn back and abandon the expedition, thus saving his child's life. The chorus's description of the sacrifice makes it clear that his action is unnatural, violating the normal pattern of family life:

And her prayers and cries of 'Father', and her maiden years they go for nothing ... she shot each of the sacrificers with a piteous dart from her eye, standing out as in a picture, wishing to address each by name, since often in her father's hospitable halls she had sung, and virginal with pure voice had lovingly honoured the paean of felicity at the third libation of her loving father. (228-9, 240-7)

If the chorus emphasise that she was young and female, it is to stress that she was defenceless and vulnerable, an unwilling victim who was denied the one retaliation left to the powerless, the curse that even her mother was able to release upon her son and murderer, Orestes. That Agamemnon's attitude would have seemed unnecessarily cruel is apparent from the story of the eighth-century B.C. Messenian king Aristodemus, who offers his daughter as a sacrifice against the Spartans in response to an oracle (Q14Fontenrose=361-2PW), but murders her first in anger to show that she is not pregnant; she is then accepted as a substitute for the sacrificial victim (Pausanias 4.9.4-9). Later in despair the king dreams of her and kills himself: 'He reckoned ... that he had become the murderer of his daughter to no purpose, and seeing that there was no hope of salvation for his country, he killed himself on his daughter's tomb' (4.14.4). In Apuleius' *Metamorphoses*, when an oracle demanded that the king place his beautiful daughter Psyche on a high cliff to become the bride of a monster, 'he moaned, wept, lamented for many days'; even though Psyche does not blame him, because she knows the blame should fall on the goddess Venus, her parents shut themselves up in their house and 'devote themselves to eternal night' (4.33-4).

Euripides, in contrast to Aeschylus, allows both Iphigenia and Clytemnestra to confront Agamemnon directly before the sacrifice. In the *Iphigenia at Aulis*, Agamemnon summons his wife and oldest daughter to Aulis, where the Greek ships are beached in preparation for their departure to Troy, on the pretext that he wishes Iphigenia to marry Achilles. But Clytemnestra and Iphigenia discover what Agamemnon's real plans are, and Iphigenia herself tries to persuade her father not to kill her. But unlike the chorus of the Agamemnon, who reflect not only on the breach of normal family ties, but on the delusion and arrogance inherent in Agamemnon's action, Iphigenia in Euripides' drama concentrates on his role as father. She clasps his knees with her body, reminding him that he begot her, and that by killing her he will separate her not only from life but from her family:

Do not force me to see what lies below the earth. I was first to call you father and you first to call me your child. I was first to entrust my body to your lap and to give and receive sweet embraces. (1220-1).

She reminds him of what they used to say to each other about the future, his hopes for her marriage and her plans to look after him in his old age, 'offering a nurse's care in return for your pains' (1230). What, she asks, has *she* got to do with the marriage of Helen and Paris (1236-7): 'Look at me, give me your face to kiss, so that I will have this as memory when I die, in case I can't persuade you' (1238-40). She asks her brother Orestes to plead for her, and while the two children stand before him, she concludes, not inappropriately to the parent who gave her life, that life is what matters, and living badly is better than dying well. This final statement echoes what Achilles says about the importance of being alive, even as a poor man's slave, when Odysseus speaks to him in the world of the dead (*Odyssey* 11.488ff.), in marked contrast to the value he attached to honour when he made his decision to die young and gloriously in the *Iliad* (18.98-9).

But later in the play, after hearing her mother and Achilles discuss what they might do to rescue her, Iphigenia changes her mind and tells her mother that she wishes to die. This time, she sees that she can save Achilles' life, since he would certainly have been killed if he had tried to rescue her, and that she can prevent her mother from being slandered by the army. Whereas in her first speech she described the world of childhood, now she is concerned primarily with the world outside herself. She will save Greece, and prevent Greek women from being carried away from their homes by barbarians, as Helen was by Paris (1377-82); she has now seen how Helen's and Paris's marriage does matter to her (cf. 1236-7). Iphigenia has, in fact, now adopted all the values of the heroic world, in which honour and shame count more than family ties or even than survival:

I shall save all these things by dying, and my reputation, because I have brought freedom to Hellas, will be blessed. You bore me for all the Greeks, not for yourself alone. (1383-6)

Why, she asks, should her one life hold back an army of tens of thousands of men? Her second major concern is for Achilles: why should he die for the sake of a woman? 'It is better for one man to live than ten thousand women' (1393-4). These lines could be taken as evidence of Greek misogyny, but it is important to remember that Iphigenia is using all possible arguments to persuade her mother not to try to fight against the inevitable. She concludes by reminding her mother that Artemis demanded the sacrifice, and that one cannot successfully oppose a god (cf. Aeschylus, *Agamemnon* 140-4; Lloyd-Jones 1983, 100-1). In the end, she wins not only the 'undying fame' (*doxan aphthiton*, 1606) that she and the great Homeric heroes hoped for, but escapes with her life, because at the last moment the goddess sends a deer to take her place at the sacrificial altar.

It is interesting that in the *Iphigenia at Aulis*, one of Euripides' last plays (*c.* 406 B.C., scholiast on Aristophanes, *Frogs* 67), the girl who accepts the values of the male world wins the greatest reward, victory for her country, glory (and survival) for herself. In other words, rather than criticise the standard ethic of Athenian behaviour towards the end of his life, as scholars continue to suppose, Euripides appeals to the basic patriotism of his earlier plays. In one of these, the *Children of Heracles* (430 B.C.; Zuntz 1955, 81-8), Demophoon, the king of Athens, can win the war against the attacking Argives, and save not only his city but Heracles' nephew Iolaus and the children of Heracles suppliant at the altars in Athens, but only if a young girl is sacrificed to Demeter. Demophoon refuses to offer one of his own children, or demand that any other citizen do so against his will, but the eldest of Heracles' daughters, Macaria, volunteers. She reasons that if the Athenians are willing to die on her behalf, she should be ready to die on theirs, especially since she is a daughter of the hero Heracles. In any case, death is preferable to the dishonour that she would suffer should Athens be taken, or if she should be forced to go into exile, where people would accuse her of cowardice and drive her away because she betrayed her friends: 'Who would want to have me as a destitute maiden or as a wife or to get children on me? It would be better to die than to end up disgraced for this, despite my noble birth' (523-6). Pausanias records the similar legend of how when an oracle demanded of the Thebans the sacrifice of the citizen of the most noble descent, 'Antipoenus, who had the most distinguished ancestry, did not care to die on behalf of the city, but his daughters were willing. So they took their own lives, and have [ritual] honours on that account' (9.17.1).

Similar arguments are put forward after the fall of Troy in the *Hecuba* by Hecuba's daughter Polyxena, who goes willingly to be sacrificed to the ghost of Achilles. Polyxena does not want to be thought to be a coward; what use is there for her to live now that her father is dead and her kingdom lost? Like Heracles' daughter, she stresses her noble birth: before she had been like a goddess except for having to die; now she is a slave. Suppose that she was acquired by a harsh master and made to be a cook or a housecleaner or the spend all day weaving, or still worse, forced to share her master's bed? (342-72). Later in the play the Greek herald Talthybius reports that, as Polyxena was about to be sacrificed, she reminded her captors that she was dying willingly, and as a free woman; she asks them not to hold her, since she would be ashamed to be called a slave princess among the dead (547-52). She undoes her *peplos*, so that her breast is revealed, and she offers Achilles' son Neoptolemus the choice of her chest or her throat, in order to emphasise that she is going to her death voluntarily, and that he could kill her as he might an enemy, rather than slit her throat as if she were an animal. Neoptolemus follows sacrificial ritual and cuts her throat, but the herald Talthybius observes that 'although she was dying, she took care to fall in a seemly way, hiding what ought to be hidden from the eyes of men' (569-70). This behaviour, provocative as it might seem to us, arouses in the Greek army who observed it only respect and pity; they bring leaves and branches to throw on her, and demand that their fellows offer something to the girl who excelled in courage and nobility (557-8). If anything, the references to her sexuality provide a grim reminder that if Troy had not fallen when it did she would have been ready for marriage. Her mother requests that no one in the army be allowed to touch her corpse, fearing that in the confusion someone might do it harm. She asks that water be brought for her to wash her daughter for the last time, not as would have been normal, before her wedding, but to prepare her body for burial, 'bride that is no bride and young girl who is young girl no longer' (612), reflecting, as so often in grave inscriptions, on the contrast between a parent's hopes and the present grim reality (above, p.51).

The notion that death was preferable to slavery would not have seemed surprising to a Greek audience. In the *Trojan Women* (415 B.C.), Andromache is prepared to kill herself before allowing herself to be possessed by a new master, and is restrained only by the hope, which soon proves to be false, that she may live to keep her son Astyanax safe in captivity. But an epitaph by the third-century B.C. poet Anyte records that in real life also maidens committed suicide rather than face rape or enslavement:

We leave you, Miletus, dear homeland, because we rejected the lawless insolence of impious Gauls [277 B.C.]. We were three maidens, your citizens. The violent aggression of the Celts brought us to this fate. We did not wait for unholy union or marriage, but we found ourselves a protector in death. (*AP* 7.492=xxiiiGP=*WLGR* 11)

Another epigram, probably by the second-century poet Antipater of Sidon, describes how a mother killed herself and her two daughters during the sack of Corinth in 146 B.C.: 'We chose a brave death ... for us the fate of freedom was better than slavery' (*AP* 7.493=lxviiGP). Pausanias records how at the same time the Greek general Diaeus of Megalopolis killed his wife, so that she would not become a captive of the Romans, and then killed himself by drinking poison (7.16.6). A pagan inscription from Paphlagonia describes how Domitilla, a fourteen-year-old girl who had been married only seven months, killed herself during the invasion of the Goths in A.D. 262-3: 'She won the crown of chastity. She was the only one of the young girls whom the [Goths] were about to violate ... who was not afraid to choose death instead of harsh violence (*hubris*)' (Lebek 1985, 7-8).

By having his characters emphasise the importance to them of the value that society throughout the Greek world placed on women's honour, Euripides makes the idea of willing death seem believable, even in a time when human sacrifice was unthinkable, and animal sacrifices were regularly offered before battles (Lloyd-Jones 1983, 88-9). In another play of Euripides where invaders can only be repelled by the sacrifice of the king's daughter, the *Erechtheus* (*c.* 423 B.C.), the king's wife, Praxithea, is moved by patriotism to offer her child willingly (fr.50Austin). Athens, she claims, with its indigenous population and its real right of citizenship is the best possible city; her children were born in order to defend their city. She would not have kept a *son* back from the fighting: 'I hate mothers who instead of honour choose that their children should live, and advise cowardice' (30-1). Instead, her daughter's one life will save many: 'O fatherland, would that all who dwell in you loved you so much as I' (50-4). In the *Erechtheus*, as in the *Children of Heracles*, the women are shown to be capable of the greatest heroism in male terms, willing, as men must be in war, to sacrifice their families and their own comfort and their very lives to fight for their country. In Euripides' *Phoenician Woman* (*c.* 409 B.C.), even though his father Creon tries to get him to escape, Menoeceus, the oldest son, willingly offers himself as a human sacrifice for his country because of patriotism and honour both:

I shall go and save my city and give my life to die on behalf of this land; for not to do so is disgraceful. The hoplites who stand in battle are not compelled by oracles or the gods and do not hesitate to die ... and if I betrayed my father, brother, and my city, I would go as a coward outside my land, and wherever I would live would seem a coward. (998-1005)

In Sophocles' dramas, family honour compels Electra, when she thinks her brother Orestes is dead, to consider killing Aegisthus herself, and Antigone is willing to risk death in order to bury her brother Polynices in defiance of her uncle Creon's edict (above, p.81).

I knew that I would die, how should I not? even if you had not proclaimed the death penalty. But if I die before my time, I count that as a benefit, for whoever lives as I do, surrounded by evils, how can he not benefit by dying? (460-4)

Antigone claims that she has carried out the wishes of the god of the dead: 'It is Hades who desires these rites' (*nomoi*, 519), and the 'rites' or 'laws' (*nomoi*) she is observing, although unwritten, were established by the gods (450-7). Creon insists that the laws laid down by men (*nomoi prokeimenoi*) must also be observed, and that she is doing violence to them (*hubrizein*, 480-1) by disobeying, and further violence by disobeying them openly and boasting of it (482-3). He suspects that Antigone and her sister Ismene are plotting his overthrow (533), and refuses to let a woman rule over him (*arksei*, 525). Both sisters 'must now be women and not unrestrained' (579), that is, like wives instead of the unmarried maidens that they are, they must be restricted to the palace. Clearly, Creon feels that giving in to a woman's wishes would be dishonourable; but his primary motive in seeing that the death sentence is carried out, even against his niece, is that a law designed for the benefit of his city had been broken. But by the end of the play the gods show that it is the law of the gods that must first be obeyed, even at the expense of human values.

Antigone says that she knows that she must die, but she does not go to her death gladly, even though she knows that she will be reunited with the family that she has kept together by ensuring that Polynices is given due rites of burial (896-902).

Instead, she laments that she has died 'without a marriage bed,
without a bridal song, without a share of marriage or the raising
of children' (917-18); i.e. what women, according to their own
words, most desired in life (above, p.51). 'Cursed and unwed'
she goes to share a home with her family in the lower world (869),
an existence that no Greek could imagine to be superior to a
happy life on earth.

Because the Greeks did not believe in a rewarding afterlife,
these mythical martyrs show a moral courage that may surpass
the more celebrated historical martyrs of the early Church. It is
interesting that in the first centuries of the Church, women
continue to be prominent among those who are willing to
sacrifice themselves on behalf of a higher cause. We must ask, as
we have for the pagan martyrs, to what extent sex was a factor in
their deaths, either in their decision to die, or in the motives of
those who executed them.

One of the earliest martyrologies, the *Acts of Perpetua and
Felicity* of Carthage, who were sentenced to death in A.D. 203,
includes what is said to be the memoirs of the martyr Perpetua
herself (Musurillo 1972; Rader 1981). Also, unlike other
martyrologies, Perpetua's tells not only about herself but about
the other members of her family (Dodds 1965, 47-53; Lefkowitz
1981, 53-4). Perpetua was a young mother with a nursing baby
when she was taken into custody; she brings her baby with her to
prison, then gives it to her mother to look after, then gets the
baby back again, to her delight: 'At once I recovered my health,
relieved as I was of my worry and anxiety over the child. My
prison had suddenly become a palace, so that I wanted to be
there rather than anywhere else' (3.4-5, tr. Musurillo 1972, no.8).
But then her father takes the baby away from her, and begs her
to give up her faith in order to return to her family, but she
refuses to take the oath of loyalty to the Emperor and make the
required sacrifice for his safety; her father keeps trying to plead
with her, and is beaten with rods by soldiers. She reports then
that the baby suddenly and miraculously no longer needed her
milk, and she adds, 'Nor did I suffer any inflammation; and so I
was relieved of any anxiety for my child and of any discomfort in
my breasts' (6.8). This narrative of a mother's concern for her
infant is unique in ancient literature, and the details about her
family make it seem the more remarkable – and painful – that
she was able to give up her child, her husband and her parents.

The usual explanation is, of course, that one's faith should
dictate the rules of one's conduct, but in most cases, as we have
seen, extenuating circumstances also contribute. Her conflict
with her father is so marked in the narrative that she appears to
some extent to be rebelling against her family (women were
married young, at about 14), and that part of the appeal to her of
her new faith was that it offered a new, more egalitarian
existence, where women and men worked together and lived as
sisters and brothers, rather than in the structure of traditional
families, where husbands and fathers could dictate where and
how women lived. It seems significant that in the last vision she
records before she is led off to her death, she dreams that in order
to fight against the devil, she becomes a man, and defeats him in
a wrestling match (10.13-14). Did her Christianity offer to her a
means of breaking out of the limiting patterns that life in the
ordinary male-dominated world had defined for her as a woman?

In a previous discussion of this martyrology, I had suggested
that Perpetua believed that her religion offered her an
opportunity to break away from the traditional patriarchal
values of pagan society (Lefkowitz 1981, 54-8). But I should have
emphasised that these patriarchal values were present also in the
early Church, and that the father whom she seeks to abandon
behaved with great kindness to her. Perpetua is shown arguing
with her father primarily because it is he, rather than her
mother, who as a man would deal with legal matters and be able
to move freely about the city; but the narrative makes it very
clear that he speaks for her mother as well. Far from having
treated her badly, he did, as he points out, actually take care of
her till she was an adult, and 'put her before all her brothers'
(5.2) – not remarkable behaviour for a twentieth-century
Western father, but particularly enlightened conduct for a
citizen of Carthage at the beginning of the third century A.D.
Most pagan societies had a high rate of infanticide, and Carthage
is the city for which we have extensive archaeological evidence of
human sacrifice up until the second century B.C., when it was
destroyed by Rome (Henrichs 1981, 205, 196nn.3, 4; Stager &
Wolff 1984, 42-4). If a man raised a daughter, and gave her
preferential treatment, he was rich, and certainly humane. Nor,
in his plea to her, does he express any attempt to order her about;
rather, he appeals to her ties and responsibilities not only to
himself but to all of her family: 'Do not abandon me to be the

reproach of men. Think of your brothers, think of your mother and your aunt, think of your child, who will not be able to live once you are gone. Give up your pride! You will destroy all of us! None of us will ever be able to speak freely again if anything happens to you' (5.2-4).

Thus Perpetua does not go to her death so much because she is a woman, as in order not to be a woman, with all the usual responsibilities to her family. The narrative reveals a desire on Perpetua's part for general rebellion against her family and her old way of life, with all that it involved. The new existence which she hoped to obtain through Christianity offered her a new family, where she still sought the approval and protection of males, but without conventional demands of sexuality and reproduction. The early Church offered recognition and opportunities for service to women, but only if they denied their sexual and reproductive functions; hence in her moment of final triumph over the devil, St. Augustine praises her in his sermons for behaving with manly courage (*Serm.* 280.1, 281.1, 282.3; *PL* v. 38). A form of liberation, perhaps, but one that is even more restrictive than the traditional roles assigned to women by the pagans.

Another interesting martyrology describes the trials and martyrdom of eight women living in Thessalonike, in northern Greece, in A.D. 304, a century after Perpetua's death (Musurillo 1972, no. 22). The story of their persecution and suffering was the basis of a little drama, *Dulcitius*, by the tenth-century nun Hroswitha of Gandersheim in Saxony (now in East Germany), who turns it into the triumph of purity and virginity over lascivious and clownish Roman persecutors. But the original martyrs were not all virgins (one was pregnant), and they were persecuted not merely for being Christians, but for what apparently struck the Romans as threatening behaviour: they had gone together to the mountains to read holy scripture. At the time, it would have been unusual for women to be living together by themselves away from their families and without the company or supervision of men (in other martyrologies devoted Christians lived together as 'brothers and sisters', like the chaste couples Paul knew in Corinth; 1 Cor. 7.29, 36-8; Meeks 1983, 102). The Romans would also have been worried by the books the women had with them, not because they considered it unsuitable for women to read, since upper-class women at least were often literate. The documents in these women's possession, however, because they were not traditional, could have seemed to the Romans seditious, or possibly even magical (Benko 1985, 114, 129). In the trial, the Roman prefect Dulcitius is reported to have said:

You have deliberately kept even till now so many tablets, books, parchments, codices and pages of the writings of the former Christians of unholy name ... Who was it that advised you to retain those parchments and writings up to the present time? ... Was anyone else aware that the documents were in the house where you lived? ... Now after you returned from the mountain where you had been, as you say, were any persons present at the reading of these books? (5.1-7)

Dulcitius could hardly have found reassuring the reply of the most prominent of the women, Irene:

As for our own relatives, we considered them worse than our enemies, in fear that they would denounce us. Hence we told no one [where the documents were] ... It caused us much distress that we could not devote ourselves to them night and day as we had done from the beginning until that day last year when we hid them. (5.3-8)

The prefect Dulcitius sentences Irene to be placed naked in the public brothel; the writings and the chests that contained them were publicly burned. It is reported as a miracle that no one touched her or even insulted her when she was in the brothel, but it is also possible that the men of the city avoided her because they thought of her as a dangerous sorceress, on account of her strange behaviour in the mountains and with the books.

How much of the persecution was directed against these martyrs because they were *women*? In the nun Hroswitha's version of this story, all traces of discrimination on Dulcitius' part vanish; he is simply lustful and sadistic, and there is no reference to the problem of the books and papers that the girls tried to hide. Placing Irene in a public brothel certainly sounds like sexual persecution; but it is interesting to note that in the original transcript of the trial she is not, like many male martyrs, tortured or beaten. By placing her in the brothel the real Dulcitius, the Roman magistrate, may have hoped to get her to abandon her faith and confess any seditious crimes she may have committed, since, for a woman of noble family, losing her

virginity in this way would mean permanent disgrace. Whether
for humanitarian or political reasons, he clearly did not want to
condemn anyone to death without ample opportunity to recant
(Lanata 1973, 220). At first he sentences only two of Irene's
comrades to death, and puts the others in jail 'because of their
youth' (4.4). To Dulcitius the notion of wishing to die for one's
faith would have seemed incomprehensible. Why would one
insist on having just one god, when there was room in the world
for many? The Greek officials in Palestine could not understand
the behaviour of the Maccabees; in A.D. 178 the Roman
philosopher Celsus claimed that Christians 'offer their bodies to
be tortured and crucified to no purpose'; that they are 'mad'
because they 'deliberately rush forward to arouse the wrath of an
emperor or a governor, which brings upon them blows and
tortures and even death' (Stewart 1984, 124).

Irene and her companions were martyred in A.D. 304. But by
the end of the century Christianity had become the established
faith in the Roman world, and pagan rites and sacrifices had
been declared illegal; now it was the pagans who were
persecuted. Hypatia of Alexandria, who was murdered in A.D.
415, was not exactly a martyr, because she did not die as a
'witness' to her faith; but we may well ask whether her death was
to some extent caused by her being a woman. In a memorable
passage, Gibbon makes it appear that the Christians behaved in
an even more brutal fashion than the Romans who had
persecuted the virgin Irene in Thessalonike. Speaking of Cyril,
the patriarch of Alexandria, Gibbon writes (1854, V 213):

He soon prompted, or accepted, the sacrifice of a virgin who professed
the religion of the Greeks ... Hypatia, the daughter of Theon the
mathematician, was initiated in her father's studies ... she publicly
taught, both at Athens and Alexandria, the philosophy of Plato and
Aristotle. In the bloom of her beauty, and in the maturity of wisdom, the
modest maid refused her lovers and instructed her disciples; the persons
most illustrious for their rank or merit were impatient to visit the female
philosopher; and Cyril beheld, with a jealous eye, the gorgeous train of
horses and slaves who crowded the door of her academy. A rumour was
spread among the Christians that the daughter of Theon was the only
obstacle to the reconciliation of the praefect [of Egypt, who has been
accused of sacrificing to the ancient gods], and that obstacle was
speedily removed. On a fatal day in the holy season of Lent, Hypatia
was torn from her chariot, stripped naked, dragged to the church, and
inhumanly butchered by the hands of Peter the Reader and a troop of

savage and merciless fanatics; her flesh was scraped from her bones with sharp oyster-shells, and her quivering limbs were delivered to the flames. The just progress of inquiry and punishment was stopped by seasonable gifts [i.e. bribes]; but the murder of Hypatia has imprinted an indelible stain on the character and religion of Cyril of Alexandria.

Gibbon's account stresses the rationality and education of the pagan woman, and the violent passions and ignorance of her murderers; he also adds details of sexual sadism: they stripped her naked, they scraped her flesh from her bones with sharp oyster-shells. The biography of Hypatia in the ancient encyclopaedia known as the Suda says simply that 'she was torn to bits by the Alexandrians, and her mutilated body was scattered through the city' (D166Adler). In this biography, it is not even clear that the murder was committed at the patriarch Cyril's instigation; civil unrest in general was said to have been another cause (Rist 1965, 214-25). Certainly her gender would have given her a certain notoriety, if only because it was very unusual for a woman to be a practising philosopher, though there had been others in the past, usually relatives of male philosophers. But unlike her pagan predecessors, she remained a virgin, and, on occasion, openly denied her femininity: she taunted an admirer with a Platonic homily that used as its object one of her sanitary towels (below, p.131); according to her biography, 'she threw a rough cloak (a *tribon*, like a man's) about herself and went forth through the centre of town and gave lectures in public to those who wanted to listen about Plato or Aristotle or the works of some other philosophers.' Women in Hellenistic and Roman times could certainly go out alone, but to go shopping, visiting, or to a festival, and not to give lectures. The third-century B.C.. philosopher Hipparchia was criticised for going around dressed like her husband and attending dinner parties with him; when she got the better of a male philosopher ˙ı a discussion about logic, he tried to pull off her cloak *himation*, Diogenes Laertius 6.97=*WLGR* 43; Schanzer 1985, 62-3). But even in the relative freedom of the late Republic, Amasia Sentia, who pleaded her own defence before a court in 77 B.C., was called 'androgyne', and Gaia Afrania, who brought lawsuits herself around the same time, was regarded as a 'monster' (Valerius Maximus 8.3=*WLGR* 205). Hypatia's biography relates that 'when she was going out as usual a large crowd of bestial men [the designation *theriodeis* suggests that they were hermits or monks, Rist 1965, 222], truly roughnecks, who knew no respect for the gods or the wrath of men, seized the philosopher and brought a great pollution and disgrace on their fatherland.' Certainly for Hypatia, as for Antigone, being a woman made her more visible and more vulnerable to criticism; but gender is only a contributing factor and not the central reason why they were put to death. We should not forget that she was not simply an educated woman but a mathematician; geometry and astronomy were confused by the ignorant with astrology. Like Irene, who was discovered with books and documents of a secret nature, Hypatia would have been suspected of being a sorceress (Rist 1965, 216).

But the principal motive, at least according to the ancient biography, seems to have been political. The biography reports that the patriarch Cyril:

When he passed by Hypatia's house, saw that there was a large crowd in front of the door, made up of both men and horses, some approaching, some going away, and some waiting there. He asked what the gathering was and why there was commotion in front of the house, and learned from his followers that the philosopher Hypatia was now giving a lecture and that this was her house. And when he learned this he was very upset, and soon planned her murder, the most unholy of all murders.

According to this account, Cyril's motive is not misogyny, but envy: she not only was drawing large crowds, possibly away from his sermons, but crowds of rich men – that is why he was upset to see horses as well as men in front of her door, since only the very rich could afford to own horses, or in fact had the leisure to listen to lectures. It is interesting to note that, in this account, Cyril does not so much resent her worship of the old gods (i.e. being a pagan), as her influence over important people, the very men whose support he needed for his church.

Thus, far more than a struggle of women against men, I now see in the documents we have been discussing a conflict between rational humane understanding and ignorant irrational insistence, where neither sex has a monopoly on either category. In the *Antigone* Creon was wrong – as the end of the play clearly shows – to insist that his niece be buried alive for disobeying his orders. The Roman magistrates who examined the Christian martyrs at least gave them a chance to go free if they performed what would have seemed to the Romans the most trivial of acts of allegiance to the emperor, something that would have seemed to them to require no more effort or commitment than an American's saying the Pledge of Allegiance to the Flag. The aristocrat Synesius of Cyrene, who later became a Christian bishop, studied with Hypatia, but other, uneducated brutal men, took her life. The biography does not state specifically whether they were pagan or Christian, or that they particularly resented women who behaved in an unconventional way; but it does indicate that the men who murdered her had no regard for the law or for traditional culture.

It is only in popular legends about women saints that sexuality becomes the dominant issue. For Thecla in the second-century A.D. Acts of Paul, as for Hipparchia and Hypatia, adopting a man's dress indicated that she had adopted a man's way of life and did not wish to be treated like a woman (below, p.131). But in narratives about later female saints who adopted men's dress, attention is carefully drawn to the sexuality the women are trying to deny. Hilaria, according to a sixth-century Coptic account of her life, dressed like a man in order to be accepted as a monk; she was known as Hilarion the eunuch, because 'her breasts were not as those of all women; above all, she was shrunken by ascetic practices nor was she subject to the curse of women' (75; Drescher 1947). Suspected of sleeping with her own sister, whom she cured of a devil, on her deathbed she reveals her true identity to the Abbot (80; cf. Patlagean 1976, 597-623). By the fifth century, sexuality becomes the cause of the death also of Thecla herself. In earlier accounts of her life, after returning home to Iconium, 'she went away to Seleucia, and after enlightening many with the word of God she slept a noble sleep' (43, Hennecke-Schneemelcher 1964, 364). But in an alternative ending to her life, which clearly refers to the grotto and relics of the fourth-century cult of Thecla in Seleucia described by Etheria, pagan doctors, put out of business by her healing of the sick, hire thugs to rape her: 'This virgin happens to be sacred to the great goddess Artemis. If she asks the goddess for anything, the goddess listens to her because she is a virgin and all the gods love her.' They tell the men they hire: 'If you can rape her, the gods and Artemis won't listen to her about the sick.' The 'evil men ... stood like lions at her grotto and banged on the door.' But Thecla knows why they have come, and as they seize her she prays to god to save her, and 'not allow my maidenhood to be violated, which I have guarded till now in your name'; the rock opens just enough to allow her to pass through, and closes again behind her (text from cod.G, in Lipsius 1891, 271-2; Dagron 1978, 48-9). If the author of this story had been better informed about Artemis, he would have realised that although she required her attendants in myth and in cult to be virgins, she did not grant them any special powers of healing. Only in Christianity does celibacy confer a superior status. But it is perhaps ironic that the new importance accorded to virginity imparts to the lives of Christian female martyrs an emphasis on sexuality that was at most tangential in the pagan world.

7

Misogyny

If, as I have tried to argue in the preceding chapters, Greek men were not afraid of Greek women, nor did they fail to give credit to women's accomplishments even in areas ordinarily reserved for men, such as politics, why at the same time did men, often with the cooperation of women, still remain wary of women in general, and continue to deprive them of full citizen rights? In recent times it has been tempting to assume that a principal reason was men's fear of women's sexuality (Walcot 1984, 46); some critics have even suggested that men were repulsed by the appearance of the female genitalia (e.g. Keuls 1985, 125-6), and so were compelled to turn for pleasure to their own sex (Henriques 1962, 45-6). But if this was the reason, the Greeks themselves did not say so; in fact, extant Greek literature, most particularly in the narratives of traditional myth, contains little that resembles the explicit descriptions of love-making in modern novels, and Greek philosophers said so little about practical sexuality that Michel Foucault, commenting on his own *Histoire de la Sexualité*, stated that 'the Greeks weren't interested in sex' (Dreyfus and Rabinow 1983, 229).

Since it is Aristotle who in his *Politics* states explicitly that 'the male is superior and the female inferior, the male ruler and the female subject' (1254b13-15), we might profitably begin by trying to discover why he considers inferiority of the female to be a state of nature (1260a11). Here Aristotle offers no direct explanation, perhaps because he assumed that no serious argument would be proposed. But it is clear from the text that he has made certain assumptions about women's behaviour. In Sparta, where women were given greater freedom than in Athens, 'the women live with every licentiousness and luxuriously'

(1269b22-3); women's insulting behaviour towards other women has caused the downfall of many tyrannies (1314b27-8). Aristotle advises that 'it is an aid to chastity' if women be married when they are older, around eighteen years of age, because 'young women are more licentious in regard to intercourse' (1335a23-5). Presumably, then, women in the best-run governments must be kept under control because they are by nature incapable of sufficient moral restraint; or, to put it the other way round, women are morally unreliable, in regard to both sexual behaviour and financial expenditure.

In this chapter I should like to examine how Aristotle in the fourth century B.C. came to accept the 'fact' of women's moral inferiority. I will try to show that, before Christian times, Greek literature was concerned not with the physical effects of passion, but with the effects of passion on reason, judgment and accordingly on action. Both men and women can be victims of passion, but women are portrayed as being more readily susceptible to the effects of passion (even) than men, and thus inevitably are considered to be potentially more dangerous. At the end of this chapter I will also try to suggest why it is that we stress in our reading of Greek texts the references to signs of gender that the Greeks themselves seem to have regarded as incidental: because an emphasis on women's physical vulnerability was introduced into Western literature from Christian doctrine and mythology in the early centuries of the Christian era.

In order to determine what men thought about women with whom they had some kind of permanent relationship, i.e. wives, rather than *hetairai* or prostitutes, we must rely primarily on the portrayal of the effects of passion in epic and drama; comedy and amusing epigrams provide explicit information about various homosexual and heterosexual practices but principally about extramarital relations or extraordinary situations, like the women's withdrawal of their sexual favours in Aristophanes' *Lysistrata* – which was, even though we are told by Foucault and others that Greek men weren't interested in sex, highly successful. I will begin, then, at the beginning, with the story of Pandora: when Prometheus tricked Zeus and stole fire for man, according to the poet Hesiod in the *Works and Days*, Zeus then devised 'a big trouble' for Prometheus and the men of the future (56); he ordered Hephaestus to mix earth and water, 'and to put

in the voice and strength of a human being (*anthrôpou*) and to
make her a maiden's fair and lovely shape, in appearance like
the deathless goddesses'. Zeus orders Athene to teach her
handiwork; Aphrodite pours golden *charis* ('sex appeal') about
her head, and cruel desires and limb-devouring cares; Hermes
puts in a bitch's mind and a thieving nature (60-8). The Graces
and Persuasion give her jewellery, and the Seasons a crown of
flowers, and Athena dresses her; then Hermes names her
'Pandora' because all the gods gave her a gift (*dôron*). She is sent
as a 'headlong trap' to Epimetheus ('Afterthought'), Prometheus' brother, who doesn't realise until it is too late that he has got
hold of something evil (68-89). The woman opens her jar and
scatters troubles and diseases around the earth; 'she devised for
men sorrowful trouble' (95). In this account, sexual appeal is
only one reason why Pandora at first seems to Epimetheus to be
something other than the evil that she is: Hermes was ordered to
put into her a 'bitch's mind and a thieving nature', and in fact he
gives her 'lies and cunning words and a thieving nature on the
orders of Zeus the thunderer'. She brings trouble to mankind
(*anthrôpoisi*) not because of her sexuality but because she is a
bitch – not exactly what we mean by the term, but as the Greeks
thought of dogs: shameless, amoral, without judgment.

In the *Works and Days* Hesiod doesn't say that all other
women are like Pandora. But in the *Theogony*, when Zeus sees
that Prometheus has given him the bones rather than the meat of
the sacrificial victim, he orders Hephaestus to make a nameless
female creature 'from whom is descended the race of women.
They live as a great pain to mortal men (*andrasi*); they do not
bear with destructive poverty but instead with abundance'
(591-3). He then compares women to the lazy drones in a
bee-hive and adds:

... so Zeus made women for mortal men, partners in harsh deeds. But he
gave another evil in place of a good; the man who escapes marriage and
the evil that women work and does not wish to marry comes to cruel old
age in want of someone to care for his old age [presumably, a son] and
though he does not lack the means of life during his lifetime, when he is
dead the heirs of a vacant inheritance divide up his substance. But for
the man who has a share in marriage and has a good and intelligent wife,
for him steadfast evil is set against good; but if a man encounters a
mischievous sort of wife, he lives with unending pain in his heart, and
the evil has no cure. (*Theogony* 600-12)

Like the archetype created by the gods, Pandora's descendants are beautiful to look at, but destructive, a 'headlong trap' (589). Pandora's daughters are also economically detrimental; they do no work; they wish to share abundance but not poverty. Even a woman 'equipped with intelligence' (*arêruian prapidessi*, 608) is only partly able to offset evil with good; the 'mischievous sort' (*atartêroio genethlês*) brings unending pain and incurable evil.

Implicit in the characterisation in the *Theogony* of the woman from whom the race of women is descended, and more explicit in the portrait of Pandora in the *Works and Days*, is the notion that a woman's physical beauty conceals from the man who wants her and the son he cannot have without her her power to do him harm. Her desirability itself is not the problem – it is simply the packaging; the trouble is caused by the presence in women of evil intent, which emerges later as openly destructive behaviour; she releases diseases upon the world, she consumes a man's livelihood. Semonides, in his satire on women, points out the same discrepancy between appearance and true nature; a beautiful woman is like a mare: she does not do any housework, but tends to her own appearance: 'a woman like her is a fine sight for others, but for the man she belongs to she proves a plague (*kakon*), unless he is some tyrant or king' (tr. Lloyd-Jones, fr.7.67-9W=*WLGR* 30). In the same way, he uses the simile of the sea to describe another woman's nature:

She has two characters (*du' en phresin noei*) ... just as the sea often stands without a tremor, harmless, a great delight to sailors, in the summer season; but often it raves, tossed about by thundering waves. It is the sea that such a woman most resembles in her temper; like the ocean, she has a changeful nature. (7.37-42)

It is this power to seem good but to bring or think evil that makes the goddess Aphrodite so potentially harmful, not her sexual attraction alone. Aphrodite, like Pandora, is not born in an ordinary way but 'grows up' (*ethrephthê*) in the foam (*aphrôi*) surrounding the severed genitals of the god Ouranus (Heaven) (*Theogony* 191-200): 'Eros (Passion) accompanied her and beautiful Himeros (Desire) when she was born and first went into the company of the gods ... maiden's soft voices and smiles and

deceptions (*exapatas*), sweet pleasure, love, and gentleness'
(201-6). The pleasures that come from sexual passion are sweet;
but deception is potentially harmful, as Sappho says in her
prayer to Aphrodite: 'Aphrodite on your intricate throne,
deathless, daughter of Zeus, weaver of plots (*doplokê*), I beg
you, do not tame my heart with pain or with anguish, but come
here' (fr.1.1-4). Aphrodite, because she is a weaver of plots, can
bring anguish even to a *woman* in love, though Sappho's
suffering, unlike the man's in Hesiod's *Theogony*, does not result
from want of food or money, but from 'cruel anxiety' and the
possibility that she may not get what she wants, unless
Aphrodite chooses to fight on her side (25-8=*WLGR* 1).

Sappho may have derived the idea that Aphrodite can serve as
an ally in a war for a woman's affections from the myth of Helen,
who, in Sappho's words,

far surpassed other people in beauty, left behind the best of husbands,
and went to Troy. She sailed away and did not remember at all her
daughter or her beloved parents, but [Aphrodite] led her astray ...
(fr.16.5-11=*WLGR* 3)

Sappho tells the story in a poem that describes her feelings about
'Anactoria who is no longer near' (15-16), whose lovely step and
brilliant glancing of her face she longs to see; but in her account
of Helen's adultery Sappho does not choose to emphasise Helen's
sexual attributes, but simply her beauty, and the way Aphrodite
'led her astray', so that she forgot all normal family ties and
loyalties. It is the power of passion to affect one's mind, to cause
one to do the opposite of what one wants or should do, that
makes the works of Aphrodite a subject for song and story. As
Semonides says at the end of his satire on women, also with
Helen in mind:

Each man will take care to praise his own wife and find fault with the
others; we do not realise that the fate of all of us is alike. Yes, this is the
greatest plague (*kakon*) that Zeus has made, and he has put round us a
fetter that cannot be broken. Because of this some have gone to Hades
fighting for a woman. (112-18)

The point is that men can easily be deceived about their
character; as Hesiod says, 'for a man wins no prize better than

the good woman, nor any horrider than the bad one' (*Works and Days* 702-3).

There is no more powerful statement of the power of passion to alter man's judgment than the *Homeric Hymn to Aphrodite*. The hymn tells the story of how after Aphrodite had led aside his mind (*parek noön êgage*, 36) so that he fell in love with mortal women, Zeus got even with her by casting 'into Aphrodite herself the desire to join in love with a mortal man' (45-6), so that she could not boast that she was superior to all the other gods and goddesses. Aphrodite goes to considerable trouble to deceive the young man Zeus has chosen for her, Anchises, who is 'like to one of the immortals in appearance' (55). She goes to her shrine in Cyprus to bathe; she dresses carefully, and then assumes the form and apperance of an unmarried maiden, 'lest he be afraid of her when he perceived her [as a goddess] in his eyes' (82-3). He addresses her respectfully, as if she were a goddess in disguise, or a nymph, but she assures him that she is a mortal woman, names her parents and says that Hermes snatched her away while she was dancing to Artemis and brought her here to be his wife; she asks only that he take her 'as a virgin and without experience in love' (133-4) to show to his father and mother. But he is so overcome by the desire she casts into him (143) that he refuses to wait; 'not even if far-darter Apollo himself shot at me from his silver bow cruel arrows – then I would be willing, woman like the immortal goddesses, having gone onto your bed to go down into the halls of Hades' (151-4).

The poet's comment, after he describes how Anchises removes the clothes Aphrodite had so carefully put on, makes it clear that he is closer to a complete change of fortune than he imagines: 'and then with the will of the gods and fate, the mortal slept with the deathless goddess, *not knowing clearly [what he did]'* (166-7). Immediately afterwards, Aphrodite herself reveals the consequences of his actions to him, but without the blandishments with which she had persuaded him, quite untruthfully, that she was not a goddess: 'Wake up, son of Dardanus; why are you sleeping so soundly? And tell me if I seem to you to resemble the girl that you first saw with your eyes?' (177-9). 'He woke up, and when he saw her he was afraid and turned his eyes aside and covered his fair face with his cloak'; he reminds her that she lied to him and begs her not to 'let me live strengthless among men, but have pity on me. For a man is not

healthy in life who has slept with the immortal goddesses'
(188-90). If Anchises means here that he is afraid that he will
henceforth be impotent, he does not say so explicitly, though he
could easily have done so. It is more likely that he has in mind
what happened to Endymion, who after intercourse with the
goddess Selene (the Moon) fell into an eternal sleep, undying and
ageless, or Tithonus, whom Aphrodite herself describes in the
hymn, who ⸜was shut up by the goddess Dawn in his room,
undying but not ageless – 'I wouldn't choose that you live like
that among the immortals and survive for all time' (238-40).
Instead Anchises is to receive the son Aphrodite will bear to him
when the son (Aeneas) is four years old, but Zeus will strike
Anchises with lightning if he reveals 'or boasts in his foolish heart
that he has had intercourse with garlanded Aphrodite' (286-7).
But Aphrodite too has been saddened and shamed by the
experience:

I will be greatly disgraced among the deathless gods for the rest of time
because of you; before this the gods were afraid of my soft voice and
plotting, with which I used to join all the gods to mortal women. My
mind subdued them all. But I shall no longer have the power to boast of
this since I have been greatly deceived, miserably, indescribably. I have
wandered out of my mind, and got a child beneath my girdle because I
went to bed with a mortal. (243-55)

Like Anchises, she was deceived and led astray, 'out of her
mind', by a desire that at first seemed beautiful but then brought
pain: 'His name shall be Aeneas because of the cruel (*ainon*) pain
I have because I fell into a mortal's bed' (198-9).

In tragedy, the poetry whose purpose it is to describe the
mistakes in judgment that lead to destruction, sexual passion is
described with the metaphors of violence that also characterise
atê, the delusion that leads men to destruction, because in
Sophocles' words, 'evil (*kakon*) seems good to the man whose
mind the god is leading toward *atê*' (Sophocles, *Antigone* 622-3).
Passion (*erôs*), says the chorus in the *Antigone*, speaking of
Haemon's love for his fiancée Antigone, is 'unconquered in
battle'; it travels beyond sea and land; no mortal or immortal
can escape it, and 'he who has it is mad (*memênen*)'; passion
makes 'the minds of the just unjust to their disgrace' (791; cf.
Sophocles, *Trachiniae* 441-4). Or, as the chorus of Euripides'

Hippolytus describes it, after they have learned of Phaedra's passion for her stepson:

Eros, Eros, who distil desire upon the eyes; you bring sweet pleasure in the souls of those whom you attack ... no missile of fire or of the stars is so powerful as the arrow that Aphrodite's son Eros shoots from his arms. (525-34)

In both these passages, as in the *Homeric Hymn to Aphrodite*, it is not the females themselves who cause the trouble, but the passion they inspire in others, and the destructive actions the passion brings about. If women are blamed, as they often are by the people whose lives are affected by passion, whether their own or someone else's, it is because their minds seem particularly vulnerable to these destructive emotions. If Clytemnestra will give all women, even good ones, a bad name, as the soul of Agamemnon claims in the *Odyssey* (24.192-202), it is because unlike the faithful Penelope, who had a 'good intelligence' (*agathai phrenes*), Clytemnestra 'devised shameful deeds'. When Nestor tells the story to Telemachus, he too keeps the emphasis on her mind: 'Many times Aegisthus charmed Agamemnon's wife with his speeches. At first Clytemnestra did not do a shameful deed, for she had a good intelligence' (*phresi ... agathêisi, Odyssey* 3.264-6). But Aegisthus sent away the bard whom Agamemnon had left to watch over her, and 'with her consent took her to his house' (272). Agamemnon, in his account of the murder, continues to complain not of her sexual behaviour but of her evil intentions:

Clytemnestra with her treacherous mind (*dolomêtis*) killed Cassandra near me. I fell to the ground, raising my hands and throwing them as I died about the sword. But she – the bitch (*kunôpis*) – stood off, and did not trouble as I went to Hades to shut my eyes with her hands or to close my mouth. So there is nothing more cruel or disgraceful (doglike, *kunteron*) than a woman who plans such deeds in her mind. (*Odyssey* 11.422-8)

The inspiration for the character of Clytemnestra in the *Oresteia* derives directly from these passages: in the *Oresteia*, as in the *Odyssey*, nothing much is said about her love affair with Aegisthus; the emphasis is rather on revenge and justice. But since Aeschylus departs from Homer by making Clytemnestra the primary killer, rather than Aegisthus, he places particular emphasis on her ability to plan and to think. Her speeches to the chorus and to Agamemnon, when she persuaded him against his better judgment to walk on the tapestries, provide evidence of her skill in saying 'much to serve the time' (*pollôn kairiôs eirêmenôn*, 1372), something less than the whole truth, and it is this ability to say one thing with great effectiveness, while meaning another, that enables Clytemnestra to take both the chorus and Agamemnon off their guard (Goldhill 1984b, 42). She herself calls attention to her intelligence; she understands the way the beacon system works better than the chorus, and complains that they in doubting her account treat her as if she were a young girl (277). It is because of this command of her intelligence and emotions that the guard at the beginning of the play speaks of her 'woman's man-counselling heart' (*androboulon kear*, 11), and she herself continually reminds the chorus that she knows more than other women (348, 590-93), not because she has become 'masculinised' or 'rebelliously' rejected the responsibilities of the household to assume a man's role in the outside world of politics (cf. Foley 1981, 151). In defending her action to the chorus (and audience), she speaks of Agamemnon as an enemy (1674), and emphasises Agamemnon's sacrifice of their daughter, Iphigenia, and his infidelity to her with Cassandra and other women, in order to give some justification for her revenge; understandably, she says nothing direct about her relationship with Aegisthus, merely calling him her 'faithful friend' (1436), and does not describe in detail how she intends to live with him, in a normally structured household, as we discover her doing in the next play, the *Libation Bearers*.

By concentrating on individual words and metaphors modern scholars have tended to emphasise sexual elements in the play (Zeitlin 1978; Humphreys 1983, 41; Tyrrell 1984, 93-100). But in using the language of the hunt to describe the murder, Aeschylus is not implying that Clytemnestra has become a man – the goddess Artemis, after all, delights in the hunt and in killing – but that she has used traps along with force, like a hunter. How else indeed could she have killed Agamemnon quickly, except with a sword? When Clytemnestra discovers in the *Libation Bearers* that Orestes has returned, she asks for a 'man-slaying axe' (*androkmeta pelekun*, 889), not because she wants (by symbolic equation) to acquire a phallos, but in order to defend herself, now that Aegisthus is dead. When in that play the chorus of libation bearers speaks of the women 'monsters inimical to mortals' who have murdered male relatives, they are not concerned that women have killed *men*, but that women have killed members of their families by *treachery*: Althaea killed her son Meleager by putting the log that was 'his fellow in age' into the fire; Scylla, 'the shameless one, as he drew breath in sleep' (620) murdered her father Nisus; Clytemnestra, in a 'daring deed plotted by a woman's mind', 'against your husband like an enemy you did go' (626-7), like the women of Lemnos, 'first among crimes'; revenge by the sword will come to all these murdering women, as Clytemnestra herself says soon after in the play, 'by guile shall we perish, just as we slew by guile' (888). The dream that Clytemnestra sent libations to avert, in which she thought that she had given birth to a snake, and wrapped it in swaddling clothes, and put it to her breast, and it drew forth blood with the milk, emphasises both that her death will come as a surprise, and that she will have been its origin. Modern interpreters have assumed that the snake suggests Orestes' maleness, and that Clytemnestra in baring her breast before him is appealing to his instincts as a man (896-8; Tyrrell 1984, 110-11; Devereux 1976, 183-203). But when in the *Iliad* Hecuba bares her breast to Hector, before he engages Achilles in single combat, it is to remind him of his obligation (*aidôs*) to his mother (22.79-82). No one has suggested, presumably, that Hecuba is trying to seduce Hector, because Hecuba did not dream of giving birth to snakes, and of course Hector is not planning to kill her, but Achilles. None the less, in the *Libation Bearers*, *aidôs* for a mother is a powerful deterrent: Orestes hesitates when Clytemnestra makes the gesture, so that Pylades dramatically must utter his only speech in the drama, to remind Orestes that it is better to have humans as enemies than the gods (900-2).

The 'wrathful hounds' (924) that Clytemnestra threatens to send against Orestes, the Erinyes that pursue him in the final play of the trilogy, have seemed in Freudian terms to represent qualities that Greek men found frightening in female anatomy (Slater 1968, 189; Tyrrell 1984, 111-12). But in the *Eumenides* it is not just Orestes and Apollo who find them repulsive but the old (woman) priestess who discovers them inside the temple. She does not think that they resemble women or even the Gorgons that she has seen in paintings of the story of Perseus; they appear to be diseased, unclean and not dressed in the white clothes women are supposed to wear when in a divine precinct (Plautus, *Rudens* 279-81):

... these appear wingless, black, altogether hateful in their ways; and they snore with a blast unapproachable, and from their eyes they drip a loathsome liquid. And their attire is such as one should not bring near to the statues of the gods or the houses of men. (46-56)

Apollo tells them to go where they belong, to the sites of murder or castration, or mutilation such as the Persians practise. The Erinyes themselves claim only to want to drive their victims mad, with a song 'maddening the brain, carrying away sense, destroying the mind' (329-30, 342-3), in order to cause their victims to destroy themselves as *erôs* or *atê* might in other contexts. Their contention, that the child is of the same blood as his mother because he was nourished by her during pregnancy (606-8), is countered by Apollo with the statement that

she who is called the child's mother is not its begetter, but the nurse of the newly sown conception. The begetter is the male, and she as stranger for a stranger preserves the offspring, if no god blights its birth. (658-61)

Apollo's argument has been considered evidence of a deep-seated misogyny inherent in Athenian civilisation, but it is important to remember that the god is speaking here as a character in a play in a context where he is acting as an advocate for a person accused of matricide; had Orestes been accused of killing his father to avenge his mother, Apollo might well have said what Aeschylus has the Erinyes say about the primacy of maternal blood ties. The role of the female in conception, of course, was not clearly understood; opinions varied about whether the female seed present in the menstrual fluid contributed to the appearance and character of the child (Lefkowitz 1981, 21; Humphreys 1983, 41). But no Athenian audience would have believed that Apollo's argument was conclusive, any more than they would have considered practical the advice of the woman-hating Hippolytus, when he suggests that men ought to be able to buy 'the seed of children' and not produce the human race from women (Euripides, *Hippolytus* 618-24). In fact, the jury in Aeschylus' drama gives Apollo and the Erinyes equal votes, and it is only because Athena, who was born from her father Zeus without a mother, casts her vote for Apollo that Orestes is acquitted.

Does the outcome then represent a defeat of female values, associated in the play with darkness, pollution, madness and death, for a more enlightened and rational order associated with male values? Not really, because the Erinyes and the ghost of Clytemnestra are not the only representatives of female nature; the maiden Athena is female too, and it is significant that she is able to persuade the Erinyes to use their considerable powers to preserve human life, rather than to destroy it. When the Erinyes threaten to 'discharge poison from their heart upon the land, and after that a canker, blasting leaves and children' (782-5/810-15), Athena, in dissuading them, speaks of their powers as if they were mental rather than physical, 'Do not discharge upon this land the words of an idle tongue' (829), '[do not] hurl against my country incentives to shed blood, harmful to the hearts of young men, maddening them with a fury not of wine' (858-60). In return for a shrine, sacrificial offerings and a seat near the house of Erechtheus on the Acropolis, they promise to protect the city of Athens, her people and her harvest. They leave the orchestra of the theatre accompanied by an escort of children and women and a company of aged women, the people who are most in need of protection because of their weakness and vulnerability.

It is significant that, because they are celibate, the Erinyes, as Eumenides ('those with good will') will be able to serve as protectors of the young they had previously been pleased to destroy. The maiden Artemis, who demands the sacrifice of Agamemnon's daughter Iphigenia, is 'kindly to the helpless young of savage lions and delightful to the breast-loving whelps of all beasts that roam the wild' (*Agamemnon* 140-3); she protects not only the young but women in childbirth, and women's wombs in general; the maiden Hecate in Boeotia in Hesiod's day was worshipped as *kourotrophos*, nurse of the young (*Theogony* 450-2). Like Athena, because Aphrodite cannot 'persuade or deceive' her, these goddesses can be trusted in ways that women subject to Aphrodite's powers to alter judgment cannot. That sexually active goddesses are not trusted with the care of the young has been taken as further evidence of Greek men's fear of women's sexuality, but it is their vulnerability to emotion that makes them dangerous, not the shapes of their bodies. The goddesses who abstain from Aphrodite have less need to resort to plots and deceptions; like Artemis and Athena in their hymns they simply go about their work, and join from time to time the company of the other gods.

It is no accident that the women in tragedy who help enact the wishes of the gods are virgins: Antigone, who cares for her father Oedipus and buries her brother Polynices, and Electra, who helps Orestes avenge the death of their father Agamemnon. To them may be contrasted one of Aphrodite's most destructive victims, Medea. Because of her love for Jason, she betrayed her father, helped to lure her brother to his death and brought about the death of Jason's uncle, again through guile, and of his prospective bride and her father, and finally of her own and Jason's children. As Euripides reminds us, her very name means 'planner and deviser' (*bouleuousa kai technomenê*, cf. *mêdomai*, 'devise'; Page 1938, 102); that her gifts were used for evil is the work of Aphrodite and her son Eros. As Jason says, Aphrodite, not Medea, is responsible for his success (526-8); modern critics have cited this statement as an example of his callousness and insincerity, but the choruses of the *Antigone* and the *Hippolytus* also blame Eros for the problems they are witnessing, and in the *Trojan Women* Helen argues (930-1), though at first not altogether convincingly (1038), that Aphrodite, not she herself, is to blame for her elopement with Paris; even Penelope in *Odyssey* 23.222-4 says 'a god' drove Helen to do it: 'before that time she had not allowed folly (*atê*) to settle in her heart'. As the chorus of the *Medea* says, after Jason leaves:

Erôtes (passions) coming in excess do not bring glory or virtue to men; if Cypris [Aphrodite] would come in moderation, no other goddess would be so welcome. Never, o queen, may you let loose from your golden bow an inescapable arrow that you have anointed with desire. (627-33)

They state conditionally the idea that Cypris might come in moderation, since it is unlikely ever to happen. The Greeks, far more than we, concentrate on the moral consequences of passion, and even in the third century B.C. it was still associated with *atê*, the delusion that leads to destruction:

Cruel Eros, great pain, great harm to men; from you come destructive strife and lamentation and wailing and other boundless sorrows that come with these; Eros, may you rise up against my enemies' children, as you threw hateful *atê* into Medea's heart. (Apollonius of Rhodes 4.445-9)

Celibate goddesses are not only more trustworthy because their judgment is unaffected by Aphrodite and the delusion of passion; like Demeter when she comes to Eleusis disguised as an old nurse, they are freed from all responsibilities connected with reproduction and so are able to look after the young and those who need them. Demeter, after Persephone has been taken from her, disguises herself as an old woman, past child-bearing and the works of Aphrodite, so that she is able, both because of her experience with children and her present lack of involvement with men, to serve as a nurse for the son of a king, Demophoon (*Homeric Hymn* 2. 202-4). She tells his mother, in a speech that sounds like an incantation, 'I know a strong antidote against the root-cutter [i.e., poisoner]; I know the good cure for painful attack' (229-30). But like Hecate who can, if she wishes, easily take away the fisherman's catch (Hesiod, *Theogony* 443), Demeter can withdraw her protection at a moment's notice. When challenged by the baby's mother for putting her child in the fire, Demeter gets angry, puts the baby on the ground (251-5), and leaves; still mourning for her lost daughter, she 'made a most dreadful year on the earth that sustains mortals, a vicious (*kunteron*, doglike) year, when the earth sent up no seed; for the goddess Demeter had hidden it' (302-7). This withdrawal of her favour, however, is not so capricious as Aphrodite's desire to sleep with Anchises, because it adheres to a recognised code, which men and gods both will know how to follow: in return for honour and respect – which includes accepting what the gods give, however strange it may seem, like putting one's only son into the fire – the gods will give their support to men. The Erinyes-Eumenides in the *Oresteia* behave like Demeter in the *Hymn*; all were goddesses connected with the regions below the earth, with death as well as with life. Demeter was also worshipped as 'Erinys' in Arcadia, because of her anger (Pausanias 8.25.5-6, cf. 8.42; Richardson 1974, 258).

But for mortal women, who did not have the power to vent their wrath on the world like the Erinyes, the honours and rewards of chastity were greatly reduced. Epitaphs lament that young girls died before they could be married, and Electra in

Sophocles' drama complains that she is not allowed to marry because her son might avenge Agamemnon's death (164-5, 187, 961-6). There was, however, some advantage in remaining celibate if it permitted access to a priesthood or temple service. The rewards of these positions varied, depending on the wealthy of the precinct, and most were hereditary, within aristocratic kinship groups (phratries), if not within families. In all periods for which we have information, temple service was virtually always temporary; office would usually be held only for a year or two. In most cases the duties of the attendants did not require residence; a woman might serve several deities at the same time. Virgin priestesses were required primarily by virgin goddesses. In myth, at least, if her priestess lost her virginity the goddess Artemis became angry: when Comaetho, the priestess and her lover Melanippus used Artemis' sanctuary 'as a bridal chamber', Artemis' wrath destroyed the people; the earth bore no crops, and there were unusual diseases and inexplicable deaths (Pausanias 7.19.2). To prevent the problem, at the sanctuary of Singing Artemis near Mantinea in Arcadia, a woman 'who had finished with intercourse' was substituted for the virgin priestess (Pausanias 8.5.12). Old peasant women were chosen for the position of Pythia at the temple of Apollo at Delphi, because being too old for intercourse with men, they were ready to serve as the 'bride' of the god (Herodotus 1.182; cf. Thuiae in *Homeric Hymn* 4.552-61; cf. Latte 1940, 9-18). But since virgins and celibates also served that most un-chaste of goddesses, Aphrodite, it seems that celibacy must have had a practical as well as a ritual function. The doctor Soranus in his *Gynaecology* recommends perpetual virginity, because women who have been prevented from intercourse by law or service to the gods, and girls who have been guarded in legal virginity 'are less susceptible to diseases because they have lighter menstrual periods and put on weight because they are spared the complications that result from ordinary life' (1.32). For widows, there would have been financial benefits, and opportunity for public honour and service: 'I was priestess of Demeter, and before that of the Cabeiroi, sir, and then of Dindymene [Cybele], I the old woman whom now the dust covers – the supervisor of many young women. I had two sons who in my happy old age closed my eyes in death' (Callimachus, Ep.48GP=40Pf=*AP* 7.728, 3rd century B.C.).

But whereas in the cults of the Greek Olympians, celibacy seems primarily to serve a practical function, in the early Christian Church (and after) it came to be considered explicitly *superior* to being sexually active – and it is here, rather than in the pagan Greek world, I believe, that the notion originates that a woman's body, rather than her mind, is vulnerable and potentially shameful. The notion that virginity (or celibacy) brings one closer to god appears first in the New Testament in the 'letter' of St. Paul to the Christian community at Corinth:

The unmarried or celibate woman (or man) cares for the Lord's business; her aim is to be dedicated to him in body as in spirit; but the married woman cares for wordly things; her aim is to please her husband. In saying this I have no wish to keep you on a tight rein. I am thinking simply of your own good, for what is seemly, and of your freedom to wait upon the Lord. (I Corinthians 7: 34-5)

The unmarried and widows of whatever age should not marry, though

if they cannot control themselves, they should marry, better to marry than to burn with vain desire (8-9) ... If, however, you do marry, there is nothing wrong in it; and if a virgin marries, she has done no wrong. But those who marry will have pain and grief in this bodily life and my aim is to spare you. (28)

In this community of Greek Christians there would have been nothing unfamiliar about the idea of celibacy freeing one for service; but it is a new idea that such service, instead of being a privilege available to a few aristocratic girls or widows, might be available to all women, at any stage in their lives.

But the universal opportunity for service offered to women of all ages and classes within the Christian community did not guarantee them a place in the hierarchy of the Church. At Corinth, a woman like Phoebe might be a ministrant (*diakonos*) and a hostess (*prostatis*) for many people, including Paul himself (I Romans 16:1), but he states explicitly that

... women should not address the meeting. They have no licence to speak, but should keep their place as law directs. If there is something that they want to know, they can ask their own husbands at home. It is a shocking thing that a woman should address the congregation (*lalein en ekklêsiai*, I Corinthians 14: 35-6).

Thus while man and woman are equal before god, or 'in the Anointed one, Jesus' (Galatians 3:28), on earth, following Jewish custom, man takes precedence (Parvey 1974, 125-8; Fiorenza 1983, 226-36). As the writer of the epistle I Timothy puts it, 'a woman must be a learner, listening quietly and with due submission. I do not permit a woman to be a teacher (*didaskein*) nor must woman domineer over man, but she should be quiet' (2:11-12); he explains, echoing Paul's own interpretation of the Old Testament story (Genesis 2:4-4:24), women must be restrained because they are by nature morally inferior: 'for Adam was created first, and Eve afterwards, and it was not Adam who was deceived (*êpatêthê*), it was the woman who, yielding to deception (*exapatêtheisa*) fell into sin' (2:13-15). Paul himself describes the serpent's deception as mental corruption, glossing 'deceived' (*exapatêtheisa*) by 'corrupt your minds' (*phtharei ta noêmata*, II Corinthians 11:3), but by the second century the serpent's deception (LXX Genesis 3.13 *exêpatêsen*) had become fully-fledged seduction. In the *Protevangelium of James*, when Joseph discovers that his betrothed Mary is pregnant, he asks:

Has the story of Adam been repeated in me? For as Adam was absent in the hour of his prayer and the serpent came and found Eve alone and deceived and defiled her (*emiânen autên*), so also has it happened to me. (13:1, PBodmer 27)

The notion of inherent female inferiority is present, though it is not so physically explicit, in the teaching of Paul. He did not approve of women in Corinth attending services, praying or prophesying, without wearing a veil (I Corinthians 11: 1-15). Pagan philosophers also approved sobriety in women's dress, but the Christian teachers differ from the pagans in not imposing similar restrictions on men. Even the oriental cults that offered Christianity such strong competition had rules of chastity for both men and women, though women, as in the pre-Christian era, had by their nature more susceptibility to pollution by blood. For example, in the cult of *Mên Tyrannus* at Sounion in the third century A.D., 'purity' for men meant being 'cleansed of garlic, pork and women'; for women, waiting 'seven days after [her menstrual period], having washed completely, and ten days after a funeral, and forty days after a miscarriage [or abortion, *phthora*]' (*SIG*³633; cf. Cyrene cathartic inscription, *SEG* IX.72=*LSCG* Suppl.115; Parker 1983, 332-51). But in early Christian doctrine, because of the danger inherent in their sexuality to themselves and to the men around them, women had a greater need for celibacy than men, not only because it offered an opportunity to serve (and be supported by) the community, but also as a means of redemption. In the apocryphal *Acts of Paul*, a popular document of the late second century A.D. that was translated from Greek into Syriac, Coptic, Ethiopic and Latin, several of Paul's beatitudes are concerned with chastity for men and women (above, p. 105), but he ends with specific advice for women: 'Blessed are the bodies of virgins, for they shall be well pleasing to god, and shall not lose the reward of their purity' (3: 5-6). Being a widow (I Timothy 3:3-15; *Titus* 2.3; Humphreys 1983, 47) and later a virgin became virtual offices within the Church. In epitaphs, where pagan virgins were said to have been carried off by Death if they died before marriage (above, p.51), Christian virgins were said to have married Christ, as in this inscription for a thirteen-year-old girl:

Here Maria has entrusted to the lamps of the saints her body; chaste, serious, wise, kind, gentle and quiet, whose high birth brought her fame in life, but by pleasing the god she surpassed the honour of her descent. For she did not choose marriage with a mortal, but in her love of virginity, an eternal marriage and with Christ sought eternal light, which is enclosed by no boundary. (*CIL* V.6734=*CE* 782; cf. Diehl 1967, no.1699=*CIL* XII.1491=*CE* Suppl.352)

Even Jesus' mother Mary, who is mentioned first in the earliest gospel, Mark, only after Jesus is grown up, and who seems to have several other sons in addition (3:31), in Matthew's gospel becomes a virgin bearer of a divine child (Matthew 1:18-25; cf. Luke 1:26-38). In Matthew, it is necessary for her to be a virgin so that the Old Testament prophecy can be fulfilled: 'The virgin will conceive and bear a son' (above, p.40). But by the second half of the second century A.D., in the apocryphal *Protevangelium of James*, Mary is discovered to be a virgin also *after* Jesus is born. The midwife proclaims to Salome, the daughter of King Herod, who happens to be standing outside the cave where Jesus was born: 'I have a new sight to tell you; a virgin has brought forth and her nature (*phusis*) is not altered' (19:3).

Salome refuses to believe, and tests with her finger, and her hand falls off, consumed by fire, only to be miraculously restored, when she acknowledges the power of God and touches the child (20:1-3).

The importance of chastity in Paul's teaching is reinforced in his apocryphal *Acts* by the story of the virgin Thecla (Hennecke-Schneemelcher 1984, ii. 353-64). The account of Thecla's adventures bears closer resemblance to an ancient pagan novel than to the doctrinal and often unexciting narratives of the canonical gospels. Thecla was engaged to a man named Thamyris, but was so inspired by the teaching of Paul that she rejected Thamyris (in the plot of a pagan novel, the heroine would simply be separated from her fiancé by circumstantial events). Thamyris accuses Paul of sorcery and has him first imprisoned and then thrown out of the city Iconium. Thecla is condemned to be burned; she is brought in naked, but makes the sign of the cross and the fire does not burn her, and God sends an earthquake and thunderstorm, and so Thecla is saved. She immediately goes to Paul and offers to cut her hair short and follow him wherever he goes, that is, in disguise as a boy. He reluctantly allows her to follow him, since she is 'comely' and subject to temptation. In Antioch, she is immediately pursued by another suitor, Alexander, but she resists him and makes fun of him, so that Alexander gets angry and has her condemned to wild beasts; but a lioness licks her feet, and Tryphaena, a rich woman who has lost her own daughter, adopts her. Alexander takes Thecla off again to the beasts, but the lioness defends her, and all the women in the audience are on her side. She is thrown in a pit full of water to be devoured by seals (*sic*), and then when she uses the water to baptise herself, she is bound by her feet to bulls (like Dirce in the pagan myth), but Tryphaena faints, and Alexander asks to have Thecla freed; the governor and all the women recognise the power of God. But Thecla leaves Antioch, dressed as a man, and searches for Paul in Myra, and he sends her forth to teach.

The author of the *Acts of Paul* makes no reference to what Paul said to the Corinthians about women keeping silent in meetings, though he seems familiar with other aspects of Paul's doctrines, the Acts of the Apostles and the first three gospels. But probably Thecla had now proved herself to be beyond temptation, because of her courage and resistance to men, to have become enough like a man to be able to do a man's work. She returns to her home town Iconium, to discover that her fiancé Thamyris is dead, but her mother alive, which she takes as a sign of the power of God: 'And when she had borne this witness she went away to Seleucia, and after enlightening many with the word of God she slept with a noble sleep' (3.7-43). The story does not so much do credit to women (cf. Dagron 1978, 38-9; Davies 1980, 58-61; Macdonald 1983, 34-53), as express the Church's restrictive and demanding notions about female conduct (Patlagean 1976, 597-623), as contrast with pagan adventure stories makes clear. Perpetual chastity is now the goal of the courageous heroine, rather than marriage. The heroine not only dresses like a man to ward off temptation, but she behaves like a man in other respects, rewarding her mother and then her surrogate mother Tryphaena with preaching instead of affection, and leaving them both behind in order to go on with her work.

The *Acts of Paul* demonstrate more clearly than any doctrinal document how distant the notion of Christian celibacy is from the pagan. Before the Christian era, no pagan celibate, even if she served for an extended term, like the Vestal Virgins in Rome, needed to be ashamed of her femininity. In the fourth century B.C. the female philosopher Hipparchia adopted men's clothing, like two of Plato's female pupils (Diogenes Laertius 3.46), but she was married to the philosopher Crates, had intercourse with him in public and went with him to dinner parties, like a *hetaera* (D.L. 6.96-8). But by the fourth century A.D., after pagan philosophers had become as ascetic as Christians, the philosopher Hypatia of Alexandria chose to remain a virgin. When one of her pupils fell in love with her, she displayed and threw before him one of the rags she used as a sanitary napkin, and said: 'You are in love with this, young man, not with [the Platonic ideal of] the Beautiful' (Suda 644.12ff.=Damascius fr.102 Zintzen). Like Thecla and the third-century Christian martyrs Perpetua and Irene, Hypatia – at least according to this anecdote – believed that in order to carry on with her work it was necessary to deny her femininity (above, p.108).

It seems clear that it is the early Christians, rather than the ancient Greeks, who first became conscious of, if not obsessed with, the dangers of women's sexuality, and that it is from them rather than Aeschylus, Euripides or Plato, that the fear of women's bodies (rather than their minds) ultimately derives.

After all, it was the Christians, and not the Greeks or Romans, who began by the late third century to worship a female divinity who was believed simultaneously to be both a mother and a virgin, the opposite of the evil Eve of the Old Testament. Only Mary, mother of Jesus, was able to join her son in heaven because she was free from the taint of sexuality, and yet able also to be a mother – the one means by which ordinary women, who gave into their sexuality, might, according to doctrine, be saved (I Timothy 2:15), provided they are steadfast in faith, love, and holiness, with chastity (*sophrosunê*). No Greek goddess ever offered to woman an ideal so impossible of achievement; at least in Greek myth, an energetic young woman like Nausicaa or Medea or even Dido might seem to resemble the goddesses Artemis or Diana, or in real life might serve them as a priestess, even if only for a little while.

Epilogue

If there ever was a time when women ruled the civilised world, or even served as the central focus of a civilised society, Greek myth does not record it; such societies, to the extent that they are imagined, are barbarian, like the Amazons or Lycians. The myths portray with sympathy the life of young women, and their fear of marriage and the separation from their own families that it will bring. But at the same time myth portrays marriage and motherhood, with all the difficulties they involve, as the conditions most women desire, and in which women can be best respected by society and happiest in themselves. On occasion, myths show women advising male rulers and even taking over some of their responsibilities; when faced with serious moral decisions, women take courageous action, even at the cost of their own lives, and win admiration. But at the same time, other myths warn of women's ability to deceive men and betray their trust, particularly as the effect of sexual passion on their minds. What the myths themselves seem not to describe, at any time or place, is the possibility of true independence for women, apart from their families or society as a whole. There are in myth no successful communities of women apart from men, or conditions in which women continuously dominated over the other members of society.

Why did the Greeks fail to imagine that a Greek society could exist in which men and women would prefer to share those responsibilities, or where women might fight and govern, while men performed the traditional duties of the wife at home? Was it as the result of a deliberate repression (French 1985, 72; Keuls 1985, 324)? Were they afraid that organised groups of women might destroy them, as the daughters of Danaus killed their husbands on their wedding night in 'the most, perhaps one of the most widely dramatised motifs in Greek culture' (Keuls 1985,

337-8)? If, as I have tried to show in the preceding chapters, we look directly at the surviving dramatic representation of the myth, and not simply at a summary of the story, Aeschylus does not seem to be advocating or even describing patriarchal repression or stratification. The Danaids have fled to Argos with their father to escape from cousins who wish to marry them against their will. Whether the girls object to their suitors personally, or to men in general, is not clear; but in either case, they have not only their father's support but his guidance: 'our father Danaus, advisor and leader, arranger of pieces on the board' (*Suppliant Women* 11-12). The king of Argos, although reluctant to involve himself in a war, offers them sanctuary. Although they themselves express a general fear of men, 'May I never become in any way subject to the power of males' (*arsenôn*, 392-3), their father and the king behave honourably and are sympathetic to their plight. The play itself thus seems to be concerned not with male-female conflict in general, but with a particular case of a disputed marriage and the issues of justice that derive from it.

In fact, Greek men may not have been so concerned with repressing women as with protecting them, in a world where women both from a physical and medical point of view were far more vulnerable than they are today. Oedipus, observing that his daughters have done more on his behalf than his sons, comments that in Egypt 'the men sit at home and work at the loom while their wives go outside and provide the means of life' (Sophocles, *Oedipus Coloneus* 340-1), as if it were unreasonable to expect women to support and care for their aged fathers when men were available. He means his remarks as a compliment; he fully appreciates what his daughters have done for him:

My sons, who ought to have struggled for me, run the household at home like girls, but you instead of them work on my behalf; [Antigone], from the time she ceased to be a child and developed her full strength, has always been a wanderer with me, poor thing, an old man's guide. Often in the wild woods without food, barefooted, journeying, exhausted by heavy rain and heat, miserable, she thinks of secondary importance the comforts of home, so her father can have sustenance. (342-52)

Oedipus does not doubt Antigone's ability to look after him, or her loyalty to him; he questions only whether it is right, while her brothers are alive, for her to live this sort of life.

If Greek men wished to repress Greek women through their mythology, why do their two most important epics, the *Iliad* and the *Odyssey*, describe a war fought on behalf of a woman? If it were only their honour they had set out to defend, after the Trojans had been punished, they would have allowed Menelaus to kill or repudiate Helen; instead Homer tells how Menelaus brought her back to Sparta and shows her peacefully and happily employed in her traditional role. The poet Stesichorus was said to have been struck blind for writing about her elopement with Paris, and in consequence told the story that a phantom had represented her at Troy, while she herself was in Egypt (192-3*PMG*).

How did the woman who had caused the deaths of so many at Troy (Semonides 7.116-17; Aeschylus, *Agamemnon* 687-90) contrive to be appreciated even by those who had suffered most on her account? Aphrodite offered her to Paris because she was the most beautiful woman in the world (Euripides, *Trojan Women* 935), but after twenty years in Troy (*Iliad* 24.765), when even a daughter of Zeus would have aged somewhat, she was respected by her in-laws Hector and Priam, and brought home to Sparta by Menelaus, not because she was the mother of sons (Homer mentions only one daughter, Hermione; *Odyssey* 4.12-14). In the *Iliad* and *Odyssey*, her most impressive quality is a direct intelligence; she recognises the goddess Aphrodite when she appears to her in disguise (*Iliad* 3.396-7), and complains of how the goddess has treated her, carrying her off to please any man she wishes to favour; she tells Paris that she wishes he had been killed by Menelaus, 'who is superior to you in strength and hand and spear' (3.431); she tells Priam that she wishes that she had died before she came to Troy with his son, 'leaving behind the people I know and my late-born child and my dear friends' (3.174-5). She speaks the last speech in the *Iliad*, lamenting over Hector's dead body, again regretting that Paris took her to Troy, and describing Hector's kindness to her – a gentleness that Homer describes also in the scene with his family in *Iliad* 6, in contrast to his effectiveness as a warrior. No one doubts her sincerity. In the *Odyssey*, home once more in Sparta, she is the model wife. Her daughter and Menelaus' son by a slave girl, Megapenthes, are being married in the same day (*Odyssey* 4.3); apparently she would have approved of the advice Euripides has

Andromache give to Hermione about going along with one's husband in his love affairs, and nursing his bastard children, so that she might do nothing to displease him (*Andromache* 221-5; above, p.70). When she enters the room, she is compared to Artemis (*Odyssey* 4.123), but like Penelope and other model wives (Lefkowitz 1981, 26, 28) begins to work in wool. She shares her husband's sorrows (184), but gives Menelaus and his guests an elixir, *nêpenthê*, to make them happy (220-1). She speaks of her time in Troy with the same regret she expressed in the *Iliad*:

The other Trojan women wept [when Odysseus secretly entered Troy and killed many Trojans], but I rejoiced, for already my heart had turned to go back home, and I lamented my delusion (*atê*), which Aphrodite gave me, when she led me there away from my dear homeland, and made me take myself from my child and my bridal chamber and my husband, who lacked nothing, neither in intelligence nor appearance. (259-64)

It is this clever and dignified Helen who in the *Trojan Women* manages to persuade Menelaus not to kill her; her argument, however unconvincing it might seem to us, reiterates what she says in the *Iliad*: Cypris gave her to Paris; 'he came as her evil genius with no minor goddess at his side' (940-1). That she survives despite his hostility is not so much a testament to the powers of Aphrodite, as Hecuba alleges (1051), but a tribute to her ability to marshal traditional lines of argument. To the Greeks, as we have seen, what makes women appealing and dangerous is not their beauty or sexuality, but their intelligence.

Notes

PREFACE

The Death of Great Pan. The story, told by Plutarch (*Mor.* 419b-d), follows the pattern of miracle reports in the New Testament; Wicker 1975, 158-9. Originally it may have been an aetiological myth explaining the ritual lament for 'the all-great' (*pammegas*, cf. *pan megas*) Thamuz (i.e. Adonis); Brenk 1977, 96n.11.

1. PRINCESS IDA AND THE AMAZONS

Matriarchal society. To Diner's reconstruction, cf., most recently, French 1985, 72: ' ... the fundamental nature of patriarchy is located in stratification, institutionalization, and coercion. Stratification of men above women leads in time to stratification of classes: an elite rules over people perceived as 'closer to nature', savage, bestial, animalistic ... '

The Athenians and the Amazons. See also Hoelscher 1973; Thomas 1976; Francis 1980.

Bachofen's influence. See esp. Cantarella 1983, 7-36; and the materials collected in Heinrichs 1975, 331-443.

Rewriting mythology and reporting history. Surely this distinction is not mere protectionism, as Heilbrun has alleged in Cross 1985, 52-3: at a cocktail party in a New England women's college, which, like Heilbrun's alma mater Wellesley, is situated on a large lake, an anonymous classics professor speaks disparagingly of the Amazons, Antigone, and ancient women generally. The murder victim's journal contains the following entry (98):

I take particular pleasure in disliking that damn classics prig: as though what the Greeks had written were somehow in danger of being betrayed by modern interpretations. It is the most durable of literatures: what do they think they have to protect it against? It is themselves they are protecting. Ancient Greek or one's own memories – in protecting them, one guards against the future.

2. CHOSEN WOMEN

30 **Women in the audience**. Pickard-Cambridge (1968, 265) accepts Plat., *Gorg.* 502d-e as evidence for the presence of women in the fourth-century B.C. theatre, but the dramatic date of the dialogue is the fifth century B.C. As Pickard-Cambridge observes (263-4), Aristophanes' jokes about audiences are too particular to be taken as positive evidence one way or the other, cf. Wilson 1982, 157-61.

37   **Caineus' metamorphosis**. Acusilaus 2*FGrHist*F22: the papyrus text *autoisieron*, 'it was not holy for them' (*POxy* 1611 fr. 1), is probably corrupt and should refer only to the maiden (Kakridis 1947, 77-80); Vergil includes Caineus, changed back to female form, as a victim of *durus amor* along with Phaedra, Procris, Eriphyle and Dido. Caineus was the subject of a tragedy by Ion and comedies by Araros and Antiphanes (cf. Maas 1973, 65). The antiquarian Aulus Gellius (9.4.15), to show that the story of Caineus was not simply a myth, cites Pliny the Elder (*NH* 7.36-7), who says he saw in Africa a woman who had changed into a man on the day of his marriage. Pliny mentions two other cases, and Diodorus Siculus several more (32.10), but it is interesting that the poet Euenus chooses for the subject of an epigram (*AP* 9.75=*Garl. Phil.*2310GP) another case of wedding-night discovery.

38   **The *Bacchae* as social commentary**. As Albert Henrichs explains in an important article (1984, 231-4), the notion that ritual has a primarily social function is relatively modern: 'Dionysus has been so drastically uprooted from his original Greek habitat and transplanted to modern regions where blood is more plentiful than wine that he might not survive. Can Dionysus be saved?'

3. WOMEN WITHOUT MEN

45 **Rape scenes** Vase-paintings concentrate on the moment of interception, but interestingly, surviving vases depict rapes by gods of young *men*, like Zeus and Ganymede, or Eos and Kephalos, as well as the rapes by gods of women; Kaempf-Dimitriadou 1979, 77-109.

46 **Gifts in return.** When Zeus carried off Ganymede to be his lover, his father Tros received as compensation for his loss swift horses that carried the immortals (*Homeric Hymn* 5.207-17).

54 **Euripides' message.** Lloyd-Jones 1983, 144-7, warns against believing that any particular character or the chorus represents the poet. None the less Vellacott (1975, 6-8) insists that conjectures about Euripides' meaning must be made in order to protect the poet's 'integrity', and that for this purpose 'the qualified student of English or European literature, even if he depends on translations for his knowledge of Greek drama, may on occasion claim to hold opinions worth the attention of a Greek scholar'. In other words, for Vellacott, the poetry of Euripides can have validity only in terms of present-day literary values.

56 **Verisimilitude in art.** Cf. Nossis *AP* 9.604=2815GP, describing a picture: 'If your little watch-dog saw you, she would wag her tail, and think she saw the mistress of her house' (*WLGR* 19); also *AP* 6.353-4; Erinna *AP* 6.352/1796GP. But men also admire verisimilitude, Theocritus, *Idylls* 1.55-6.

57 **The meaning of the Thesmophoria.** Zeitlin (1982, 144-7), by a series of ingenious assocations, deduces that the pigs sacrificed at the festival represent the vulva (cf. above, p.26), and that the rites represent a formalised and temporary return to a matriarchal state. But it is interesting that even when women band together in Aristophanes' *Lysistrata* it is for the salvation of the community; they wish to return to their men and their normal lives (below, p.85). One wishes we knew more about Pherecrates' *Tyrannis*, where some kind of temporary gynaeco-cracy may have been involved; fr.143K.

59 **The Pythia.** It seems particularly significant that Apollo's priestess is female, since gods usually have priests of the same sex as themselves; Latte 1940, 15; Burkert 1985, 117.

4. WIVES

61 **Women poets.** Sappho's descriptions of love and loss seem to offer little grounds for Pomeroy's claim (1975, 52) that 'the lyric poems of the female writers of the Archaic Age give us the happiest picture of women in Greek literature'. Pomeroy's account of these writers is singled out for comment and splendidly garbled by French (1985, 143), in a paragraph that illustrates the risks involved in writing about the ancient world without knowledge of its languages or history:

The great Sappho had students, at least one of whom, Erinna, wrote poetry that her male contemporaries considered as good as Homer's. A group of women poets called the 'nine Earthly Muses' were viewed as the best poets of their age.

Not only did Sappho (sixth century B.C., Lesbos) and Erinna (fourth century B.C., Telos) live at different times and places; the 'nine Muses that Earth bore' were never seen together, but were only listed together in an epigram by the first-century B.C. poet Antipater of Thessalonica (*AP* 9.26=19 *Garl. Phil.*): Praxilla, Moero, Anyte, Sappho (whom Antipater calls 'the female Homer'), Telesilla, Corinna, Nossis, and Myrtis (*WLGR* 1-20). No ancient critic that I can discover compares Erinna to Homer.

63   **Penelope.** Wives are frequently compared to Penelope on grave inscriptions (Peek 165, 163-4).

69   **Provisions for wives in wills.** See also Pasion's will in Demosthenes 45.28=*WLGR* 66; Aristotle's will in Diogenes Laertius 5.11-61=*WLGR* 67. Cf. also the concept of *patria potestas* in Roman law (Treggiari 1982, 34-44).

76   **Domestic virtues.** Cf. 'Turia' 1.30: 'Why should I mention your domestic virtues, chastity, obedience, compatibility, industry in working wool, religion without superstition, sobriety of attire, modesty of appearance?' (Lefkowitz 1981, 28-9). The unique *domiseda* occurs in *CIL* VI.11602 (Comfort 1960, 275).

5. INFLUENTIAL WOMEN

81   **Antigone's politics.** Heilbrun (1973, 10) cites an unidentified verse translation: 'But to defy the State – I have no strength for that.' The Greek says only 'Do you intend to bury him, when Creon has forbidden it?' (Sophocles, *Antigone* 47).

32 **Women's role in burial of the dead.** According to Plutarch (*Moralia* 259d) Mithridates (first century B.C.) decreed that the corpse of his enemy Poredorix be left unburied, but when the guards arrested a woman burying the body, Mithridates permitted her to complete the burial and gave her clothes for the corpse, 'probably because he realised that the reason behind it was love'.

33 **Blood relatives.** Alcmena refuses to sleep with her husband Amphitryon until he has avenged her brothers' deaths (*Shield* 15-17). Intaphernes' wife chooses to have her brother spared rather than her husband (Herodotus 3.119.6), and Althaea brings about the death of her son Meleager because he killed her brothers (Bacchylides 5.136-44). The 'illogicality' (in modern terms) of Antigone's argument and its similarity to the Herodotean passage have caused scholars to question its authenticity (e.g., most recently, Winnington-Ingram 1980, 145 n.80); but cf. Lefkowitz 1981, 5n.8; Humphreys 1983, 67.

34 **Permissible action.** Humphreys' assertion (1983, 62) that 'the heroines of fifth-century B.C. tragedy are different [from the heroines of epic, like Andromache]: they are agents in their own right, acting in opposition to men or as substitutes for them' ignores the crucial distinction between right and wrong action. Althaea, for example, is listed first in a catalogue of evil women by the (female) chorus of Aeschylus, *Libation Bearers* 603ff.

36 **Melanippe the wise.** According to the Aristophanes scholia, the play provided later writers with many quotations both for and against women (e.g. frs.497-9, 502, 503N).

7 **Women in Sparta.** Redfield (1978, 160), by analysing the condition of Spartan women in terms of the artificial polarities of *oikos* and *polis*, suggests that 'we can see the Spartan policy as a somewhat extreme enactment of general Greek ideas'; but surely Aristotle regarded it as anomalous, and ultimately self-destructive. On women's status in the *polis*, see Gould 1980, 46.

7 **Cornelia.** See Plutarch, *Gracch.* 2.19; Cicero, *Brut.* 58.211; Seneca, *de Cons.* 16; Tacitus, *Dial* 28; Valerius Maximus 4.4 praef.=*WLGR* 145-9.

7 **Telesilla.** The second-century A.D. traveller Pausanias saw a statue of her in Argos (ii.20.8-10). Cf. the male poets Solon of Athens and Tyrtaeus of Sparta, both of whom were assumed to have been generals, perhaps because of the hortatory stance they adopt in their poems (Lefkowitz 1981b, 38, 42). In part, the story of Telesilla appears to be an aetiology for the annual Argive festival of Impudence (*hubristika*), one of several Greek rituals involving transvestism and role-change (Burkert 1985, 259, 440n.53). Cf. how an Argive woman was celebrated for killing king Pyrrhus when he attacked the city in 271 B.C. (Stadter 1965, 52).

88   **Women's dedications.** Cf. also Pleket 15=*WLGR* 151, and *CIL* viii.23888; also Van Bremen 1981, 223-41.

90   **Berenice.** Callimachus (in Catullus' translation, 66.25-6) may have been alluding to how she helped assassins dispose of her first husband Demetrius (her mother's lover, whose presence kept her mother in power) so that she could marry Ptolemy (Justin 26.3).

90   **The male consort.** Cleopatra's daughter Cleopatra Selene issued coins in her own name, but with her husband Juba on the reverse; Macurdy 1932, 225.

90   **Lentulus' wife.** Probably she was Sulpicia, wife of Cornelius Lentulus Cruscello; Valerius Maximus 6.6.3; *RE* IV (1901) 1384.

94   **The female intercessor.** Antonina is alleged to have got her husband Belisarius' life spared through Theodora's intervention; Procopius, *Secret History* 4. Perhaps one reason why Theodora's contemporaries (like Cleopatra's) disliked her is that she often seemed to function literally as well as figuratively as co-ruler; oaths, for example, were sworn to Justinian and Theodora jointly (Gibbon 1854, iv.40); cf. also her speech in the Hippodrome (Browning 1971, 112).

6. MARTYRS

98   **Achilles' choice.** The passage from *Iliad* 18.98-9 is also cited by Plato in defence of Socrates' decision not to alter his behaviour even at the risk of execution, *Apology* 28c-d.

100   **Offering the sacrifice.** Cf. Aristodemus (above, p.96), who murders his daughter by stabbing her in the chest and in the stomach (to show she wasn't pregnant; Pausanias 4.13.2).

104   **Child sacrifice in Carthage.** In 310 B.C. two hundred children from the best families were sacrificed when Carthage was besieged, and three hundred other children 'who were

suspect' also volunteered (Diodorus Siculus 20.14; Burkert 1981, 105n.2, 121n.1)

Hroswitha. Latin text, ed. K. Strecker (Leipzig 1906); Eng. translation, L. Bonfante (New York 1979).

Sexual pollution. In Apuleius' *Metamorphoses*, Lucius the Ass is afraid to have intercourse with a murderess because of the contagion he might incur from her (*scelerosae mulieris contagio macularier*, 10.29,34).

7. MISOGYNY

Dogs. Cf. Semonides 7.12-20, with Lloyd-Jones's (1975) note on 1.12.

Women as economic liability. Hesiod (*Works and Days* 373-4) warns against the woman who wiggles her hips in order to get a man to let her poke into his granary, which also suggests that men did not always give women enough to eat; West 1978, 251. Cf. Arthur 1973, 47, who imagines that the poets' complaints are 'part of the bourgeois polemic against aristocratic luxury'. But it is hard to see why the poets ought to be considered bourgeois; see de Ste. Croix (1981, 60-2) on the meaning of Marx's terminology and the difficulty of applying it to the ancient world.

Impotence. Cf. the curse Phoenix's father places on Phoenix, that because he slept with his father's mistress he shall never have a son of his own (*Iliad* 9.554-6); for speculation that the myth reflects fear that intercourse with goddesses will cause impotence, cf. Devereux 1982, 33.

Modern emphasis on sexuality. Cf. Goldhill (1984b, 33, 195) who appears to regard the trilogy as a complex meditation on symbolism of the primal scene:

The organising of the relation of the internal ties of the *oikos* to the city constitutes the teleology of the genealogical myth (and we saw many plays on origins as explanations, linking narrative and language to sexuality through the metaphors of birth and descent – as the logoi of the trial itself turn on the sexual distinction of the origin of parentage). But this is a teleology which, as the search for and postulation of a single parent could not avoid the doubleness of parentage within the sexual opposition, cannot avoid, despite the weighty teleology of the *trilogy* itself, a continuing doubling and opposition. The telos of closure is resisted in the continuing play of difference. (283)

130   **Sexual deprivation.** Cf. how in the apocryphal *Acts of Peter*,
          when Agrippa's concubines and his wife Xanthippe refuse to
          sleep with him because they have taken the Christian vow of
          purity, Peter is executed (33-6; Hennecke-Schneemelcher 1964,
          316-18).

131   **Plato's female pupils.** Diogenes Laertius lists 'Lastheneia of
          Mantinea and Axiothea of Phlius, who is reported by
          Dicaearchus to have worn men's clothes' (3.46). According to
          POxy 3656, one of them, probably Lastheneia, studied
          philosophy first with Plato, then with Speusippus (Diogenes
          Laertius 4.2), and then with Menedemus; according to
          Aristophanes the Peripatetic 'she was pretty and full of
          unaffected charm'.

Bibliography

Adam 1963   Adam, J. *The Republic of Plato*, ed. 2. Cambridge.

Adler 1967   Adler, A. *Suidae Lexicon*. Leipzig.

Alexiou 1974   Alexiou, M. *The Ritual Lament in Greek Tradition*. Oxford.

Annas 1981   Annas, J. *An Introduction to Plato's Republic*. Oxford.

AP   *Anthologia Palatina*

Arthur 1973   Arthur, M. 'Early Greece: origins of the Western attitude toward women', *Arethusa* 6 (1973) 7-58.

Auerbach 1978   Auerbach, N. *Communities of Women: an idea in fiction*. Cambridge, Mass.

Austin   Austin, C. *Nova Fragmenta Euripidea in Papyris Reperta*. Berlin 1968.

Bachofen 1967   Bachofen, J.J. *Myth, Religion, and Mother Right: Selected Writings*, tr. R. Mannheim. Princeton.

Balsdon 1962   Balsdon, J.P.V.D. *Romen Women: their history and habits*. London.

Bamberger 1973   Bamberger, J. 'The myth of matriarchy', in *Women, Culture, and Society*, ed. M.Z. Rosaldo and L. Lamphere. Stanford: 263-80.

Barnes 1968   Barnes, T.D. 'Pre-Decian Acta Martyrum', *Journ. Theol. Stud.* n.s.19 (1968): 509-31=*Early Christianity and the Roman Empire* (London 1984) ch.1.

Benko 1985   Benko, S. *Pagan Rome and the Early Christians*. London.

Bernardini 1983   Bernardini, P.S. *Mito e attualità nelle odi di Pindaro*. Rome.

Bloch 1945   Bloch, H. 'The last Pagan revival in the West', *Harvard Theol. Rev.* 38 (1945): 199-244.

Bloch 1963   Bloch, H. 'The Pagan revival in the West at the end of the fourth century', in Momigliano 1963: 193-218.

Boardman 1982 Boardman, J. 'Heracles, Theseus, and Amazons', *The Eye of Greece*, edd. D.C. Kurtz and B. Sparkes (Festschrift M. Robertson). Cambridge: 1-28.

Bremmer 1985 Bremmer, J.N. 'La donna anziana', *Le Donne in Grecia*, ed. G. Arrigoni. Bari: 275-98.

Brenk 1977 Brenk, F.E. *In Mist Apparelled: religious themes in Plutarch's Moralia and Lives*. Leiden.

Brown 1972 Brown, P. *Religion and Society in the Age of Augustine*. London.

Browning 1971 Browning, R. *Justinian and Theodora*. New York.

Burkert 1966 Burkert, W. 'Kekropidensage und Arrhephoria', *Hermes* 94 (1966): 1-25.

Burkert 1979 Burkert, W. *Structure and History in Greek Mythology and Ritual*. (Sather Classical Lectures 47). Berkeley.

Burkert 1981 Burkert, W. 'Glaube und Verhalten', *Entretiens Hardt* 27 (1981) 91-125.

Burkert 1983 Burkert, W. *Homo Necans*, tr. P. Bing. Berkeley.

Burkert 1985 Burkert, W. *Greek Religion*, tr. J. Raffan. Oxford.

Calame 1977 Calame, C. *Les Choeurs de jeunes filles en grèce archaïque*. Rome.

Cameron & Kuhrt 1983 Cameron, A. and Kuhrt, A. *Images of Women in Antiquity*. London.

Campbell 1964 Campbell, J.K. *Honour, Family, and Patronage*. Oxford.

Campbell 1967 Campbell, J. 'Introduction' to Bachofen 1967: xi-lvii.

Cantarella 1981 Cantarella, E. *L'Ambiguo Malanno*. Rome.

Cantarella 1983 Cantarella, E. 'Johann Jacob Bachofen', in J.J. Bachofen, *Introduzione al Diritto Materno*. Rome 1983.

Cartledge 1981 Cartledge, P. 'Spartan wives: liberation or licence', *Classical Quarterly* 31 (1981): 84-105.

CE Buecheler, F. and Lommatzsch, E. *Carmina Latina Epigraphica*. Leipzig 1897-1926.

Chesler 1973 Chesler, P. *Women and Madness*. New York.

Ciccotti 1985 Ciccotti, E. *Donne e Politica negli ultimi anni della Repubblica Romana*, ed. E. Cantarella (*Antiqua* 33). Naples.

CIL *Corpus Inscriptionum Latinarum*.

CMG *Corpus Medicorum Graecorum*.

Cole 1981   Cole, S.G. 'Could Greek women read and write?' in Foley 1981: 219-46.

Comfort 1960   Comfort, H. *Am. Journ. Archaeol.* 64 (1960): 275.

Cross 1985   Cross, A. *Sweet Death, Kind Death.* New York.

DK   Diels, H. and Kranz, W., eds. *Die Fragmente der Vorksokratiker.* Berlin 1954.

Dagron 1978   Dagron, G. *Vie et miracles de Sainte Thècle.* Subsidia Hagiographica 62. Brussels.

Daube 1972   Daube, D. *Civil Disobedience in Antiquity.* Edinburgh.

David 1976.   David, T. 'La Position de la femme en Asie Centrale', *Dialogues d'Histoire Ancienne* 2 (1976): 129-62.

Davies 1980   Davies, S. *The Revolt of the Widows.* Carbondale.

de Ste. Croiz 1981   de Ste. Croix, G.E.M. *The Class Struggle in the Ancient Greek World.* London.

Delcourt 1959   Delcourt, M. *Oreste et Alcmeon.* Paris.

Detienne 1977   Detienne, M. *The Gardens of Adonis.* tr. J. Lloyd. London.

Devambez 1981   Devambez, P. 'Amazones', *Lexicon Iconographique Mythol. Grecque* (1981): 636-43.

Devereux 1976   Devereux, G. *Dreams in Greek Tragedy.* Berkeley.

Devereux 1982   Devereux, G. *Femme et Mythe.* Paris.

Diehl 1967   Diehl, E. *Inscriptiones Latinae Christianae Veteres,* suppl. J. Moreau and H. -I. Marrou. Dublin.

Diner 1965   Diner, H. *Mothers and Amazons: the first feminine history of culture,* ed. and tr. J.P. Lundin. New York.

Dodds 1965   Dodds, E.R. *Pagan and Christian in an Age of Anxiety.* Cambridge.

Drescher 1947   Drescher, J. *Three Coptic Legends. Annales du Service des antiquités d' Egypte,* cah. 4. Cairo.

Dreyfus & Rabinow 1983   Dreyfus, H.L. and Rabinow, P., 'On the genealogy of ethics', in *Michel Foucault,* ed. 2. Chicago.

duBois 1979   duBois, P. 'On horse/men, Amazons, and endogamy', *Arethusa* 12 (1979) 35-49.

duBois 1982   duBois, P. *Centaurs and Amazons: women and the pre-history of the Great Chain of Being.* Ann Arbor.

FGE   Page, D.L., *Further Greek Epigrams.* Cambridge 1981.

FGrHist. Jacoby, F. *Die Fragmente der griechischen Historiker.* Berlin 1923 – .

Fiorenza 1983   Fiorenza, E.S. *In Memory of Her.* New York.

148   *Bibliography*

Foley 1975 Foley, H. 'Sex and state in Ancient Greece', *Diacritics* 5.4 (1975): 31-6.
Foley 1981   Foley, H. *Reflections of Women in Antiquity.* New York.
Fontenrose 1978   Fontenrose, J. *The Delphic Oracle.* Berkeley.
Fraenkel 1962   Fraenkel, E. *Aeschylus Agamemnon.* Oxford.
Francis 1980   Francis, E.D. 'Greeks and Persians: the art of hazard and triumph', *Ancient Persia: the art of an empire,* ed. D.Schmidt-Bessert. Malibu.
Frankfort 1977   Frankfort, R. *Collegiate Women: domesticity and career in turn-of-the-century America.* New York.
Frazer 1921   Frazer, J.G. *Apollodorus.* Loeb Classical Library. London.
French 1985   French, M. *Beyond Power.* New York.
Friedlaender & Hoffleit 1948   Friedlaender, P. and Hoffleit, F. *Epigrammata.* Berkeley.
GP   Gow, A.S.F. and Page, D.L. *The Greek Anthology: Hellenistic Epigrams.* Cambridge 1965.
Gallo 1984   Gallo, L. 'La donna greca e la marginalità', *Quad. Urbinati Cult. Class.* 18 (1984): 7-51.
Garland 1985 Garland, R. *The Greek Way of Death.* London/Ithaca.
Garl.Phil.   Gow, A.S.F. and Page D.L., *The Garland of Philip.* Cambridge 1968.
Gibbon 1776-86   Gibbon, E. *The History of the Decline and Fall of the Roman Empire.* London.
Girard 1977   Girard, R. *Violence and the Sacred,* tr. P. Gregory. Baltimore.
Glasscock 1975   Glasscock, J. *Wellesley College 1875-1975. A Century of Women.* Wellesley.
Goldhill 1984   Goldhill, S. 'Exegesis: Oedipus (R)ex', *Arethusa* 17 (1984): 177-200.
Goldhill 1984b   Goldhill, S. *Language, Sexuality, Narrative: the Oresteia.* Cambridge.
Gordon 1977   Gordon, A.E. 'Who's who in the Laudatio Turiae', *Epigraphica* 39 (1977): 7-12.
Gould 1980   Gould, J. 'Law, custom, and myth', *Journal of Hellenic Studies* 100 (1980): 39-42.
Graham 1984   Graham, A.J. 'Religion, women and Greek colonization', *Centro Ricerche e Documentazione sull' Antichità Classica,* Atti XI (U.S. 1, 1980-81). Rome 1984: 293-314.

Gressmair 1966   Gressmair, E. *Das Motiv der Mors Immatura.* Innsbruck.

Hansen 1983   Hansen, P.A. *Carmina Epigraphica Graeca.* Berlin.

Harvey 1973   Harvey, A.E. *A Companion to the New Testament.* Oxford/Cambridge.

Heilbrun 1973   Heilbrun, C. *Towards a Recognition of Androgyny.* New York.

Heilbrun 1979   Heilbrun, C. *Reinventing Womanhood.* New York.

Heiler 1977   Heiler, F. *Die Frau in den Religionen der Menschheit.* Berlin.

Heinrichs 1975   Heinrichs, H.J. *Materialien zu Bachofens 'Das Mutterrecht'.* Frankfort/Main.

Hennecke-Schneemelcher 1964   Hennecke, E. *New Testament Apocrypha,* ed. W. Schneemelcher. Philadelphia.

Henrichs 1981   Henrichs, A. 'Human sacrifice in religion: three case studies', *Entretiens Hardt* 27 (1981) 198-208.

Henrichs 1984   Henrichs, A. 'Loss of self, suffering, violence', *Harvard Stud. in Class Philol.* 88 (1984): 205-40.

Henriques 1964   Henriques, F. *Love in Action: the sociology of sex.* London.

Hoelscher 1973   Hoelscher, T. *Griechische Historienbilder des 5 und 4 Jahrhunderts.* Beitraege zur Archaeologie 6. Würzburg.

Horsfall 1982   Horsfall, N. 'Allia Potestas and Murdia: two Roman women', *Anc. Soc.* (Macquarie Univ.) 12.2 (1982): 27-33.

Horsfall 1983   Horsfall, N. 'Some problems in the "Laudatio Turiae" ', *Bull. Inst. Class. Studies* 30 (1983): 85-98.

How & Wells 1912   How, W.W. and Wells, J. *A Commentary on Herodotus.* Oxford.

Humphreys 1983   Humphreys, S. *The Family, Women and Death: Comparative Studies.* London.

IG   Inscriptiones Graecae. 1873-.

ILS   Dessau, H., ed. Inscriptiones Latinae Selectae. Chicago 1979-80.

Jacob 1963   Jacob, H.E. *Felix Mendelssohn and His Times.* Englewood Cliffs, N.J.

Jacoby 1949   Jacoby, F. *Atthis.* Oxford.

Jebb 1900   Jebb, R.C. *Sophocles, Antigone,* ed. 3. Cambridge.

150   *Bibliography*

K   Kock, T. *Comicorum Atticorum Fragmenta,* Leipzig 1880.

Kaempf-Dimitriadou 1979   Kaempf-Dimitriadou, S. *Die Liebe der Goetter in der attischen Kunst der 5 Jhdt.* Basel.

Kaibel   Kaibel, G. *Epigrammata Graeca.* Berlin 1878.

Kakridis 1947   Kakridis, J.T. 'Caeneus', *Classical Review* 61 (1947): 77-80.

Kannicht 1969   Kannicht, R. *Euripides Helena.* Heidelberg.

Keuls 1985   Keuls, E.C. *The Reign of the Phallus.* New York.

King 1983   King, H. 'Bound to bleed: Artemis and Greek women', in Cameron and Kuhrt 1983: 109-27.

Kleinbaum 1983   Kleinbaum, A.W. *The War Against the Amazons.* New York.

Knox 1978   Knox, B.M.W. *Word and Action.* Baltimore.

Kurtz & Boardman 1971   Kurtz, D.C. and Boardman, J. *Greek Burial Customs.* London.

Kurtz 1975   Kurtz, D.C. *Athenian White Lekythoi.* Oxford.

L   Littré, M.P.E. *Oeuvres Complètes d'Hippocrate.* Paris 1839-61.

Lacey 1968   Lacey, W.K. *The Family in Classical Greece.* London [Reprint: Auckland 1980].

Lanata 1973   Lanata, G. *Gli atti dei martiri come documenti processuali.* Milan.

Latte 1940   Latte, K. 1940. 'The coming of the Pythia', *Harvard Theol. Rev.* 33:9-18.

Lattimore 1962   Lattimore, R. *Themes in Greek and Latin Epitaphs.* Urbana.

Leach 1969   Leach, E. 'Virgin birth', *Genesis and Other Essays.* London.

Lebek 1985   Lebek, W.D. 'Das Grabepigramm auf Domitilla', *Zeitschrift fuer Papyrologie und Epigraphik* 59 (1985): 7-8.

Lefkowitz 1981   Lefkowitz, M.R. *Heroines and Hysterics.* London/New York.

Lefkowitz 1981b   Lefkowitz, M.R. *The Lives of the Greek Poets.* London/Baltimore.

Lefkowitz & Fant 1982   Lefkowitz, M.R. & Fant, M.B. *Women's Life in Greece and Rome.* London/Baltimore 1982.

Lévi-Strauss 1955   Lévi-Strauss, C. 'The structural study of myth', in *Myth: a symposium,* ed. T. Sebeok. Bloomington 1955: 81-106.

Lewin 1966   Lewin, J. *Aeschylus: the House of Atreus.* Minneapolis.

Lipsius 1891 Lipsius, R.A. *Acta Apostolorum Apocrypha.* Berlin.

Lloyd-Jones 1964 Lloyd-Jones, H. 'A fragment of New Comedy: P. Antinoopolis 15', *Journal of Hellenic Studies* 84 (1964): 21-34.

Lloyd-Jones 1971 Lloyd-Jones, H. *The Justice of Zeus.* Berkeley.

Lloyd-Jones 1975 Lloyd-Jones, H. *Females of the Species.* London.

Lloyd-Jones 1978 Lloyd-Jones, H. 'Ten notes on Aeschylus, *Agamemnon'*, *Dionysiaca* (Festschrift D.L. Page). Cambridge: 45-61.

Lloyd-Jones 1982 Lloyd-Jones, H. *The Oresteia.* London.

Lloyd-Jones 1983 Lloyd-Jones, H. 'Artemis and Iphigenia', *Journal of Hellenic Studies* 103 (1983): 87-102.

Loraux 1978 Loraux, N. 'Sur la race des femmes et quelques-uns de ses tribus', *Arethusa* (1978) 43-85.

LP Lobel, E. and Page, D. *Poetarum Lesbiorum Fragmenta.* Oxford 1955.

LSCG Sokolowski, F. *Lois sacrées des cités grecques.* Paris 1969.

MW Merkelbach, R. and West, M.L. *Fragmenta Hesiodea.* Oxford 1967.

Maas 1973 Maas, P. *Kleine Schriften.* Munich.

MacDonald 1983 MacDonald, D.R. *The Legend and the Apostle: the battle for Paul in story and canon.* Philadelphia.

Macurdy 1932 Macurdy, G.H. *Hellenistic Queens.* Baltimore.

Mazzolani 1982 Mazzolani, L.S. *Una Moglie.* Palermo.

Meeks 1983 Meeks, W.A. *The First Urban Christians.* New Haven.

Merck 1978 Merck, M. 'The city's achievements, the patriotic Amazonomachy and Ancient Athens', *Tearing the Veil,* ed. S. Lipschitz. London.

Millar 1977 Millar, F. *The Emperor in the Roman World, 31 B.C.-A.D. 337.* London.

Millett 1970 Millett, K. *Sexual Politics.* New York.

Momigliano 1963 Momigliano, A. *The Conflict between Paganism and Christianity in the Fourth Century.* Oxford.

Musurillo 1972 Musurillo, H. *The Acts of the Christian Martyrs.* Oxford.

N   Nauck, A. *Tragicorum Graecorum Fragmenta.* Leipzig.

O'Brien 1977   O'Brien, J.V. *Bilingual Selections from Sophocles' Antigone.* Carbondale 1889.

Page 1938   Page, D.L. *Euripides Medea.* Oxford.

Parker 1983   Parker, R. *Miasma: pollution and purification in early Greek religion.* Oxford.

Parvey 1974   Parvey, C.F. 'The theology and leadership of women in the New Testament', *Religion and Sexism,* ed. R. Ruether. New York: 117-49.

Patlagean 1976   Patlagean, E. 'L'Histoire de la femme déguisée en moine et l'évolution de la sainteté feminine à Byzance', *Studi Medievali* 17 (1976): 597-623.

Peek   Peek, W. *Griechische Vers-Inschriften.* Berlin 1955.

Peek 1965   Peek, W. 'Die Penelope der Ionerinnen', *Ath. Mitteil.* 80 (1965): 163-4.

Pembroke 1965   Pembroke, S. 'The last of the matriarchs: a study in the inscriptions of Lycia', *Journ. of the Economic and Social History of the Orient* 8 (1965): 217-47.

Pembroke 1967   Pembroke, S. 'Women in charge', *Journ. Warburg and Courtauld Inst.* 30 (1967): 1-35.

Pembroke 1970   Pembroke, S. 'Locres et Tarente', *Ann. Econ., Soc. Civ.* 25 (1970): 240-70.

Pf.   Pfeiffer, R. *Callimachus.* Oxford 1949-53.

Pickard-Cambridge 1968   Pickard-Cambridge, A. *The Dramatic Festivals of Athens.* ed.2 J. Gould & D.M. Lewis. Oxford.

Pleket 1969   Pleket, H.W. *Texts on the Social History of the Greek World, Epigraphica.* vol. II. Leiden.

PMG   Page, D.L. *Poetae Melici Graeci.* Oxford 1962.

Poliakoff 1982   Poliakoff, M. *Studies in the Terminology of the Greek Combat Sports.* Beitraege zur Klass. Philol. 146. Koenigstein.

Pomeroy 1975   Pomeroy, S.B. *Goddesses, Whores, Wives, and Slaves.* New York.

Pomeroy 1981   Pomeroy, S.B. 'Women in Roman Egypt', in Foley, 1981.

Pomeroy, 1985   Pomeroy, S.B. *Women in Hellenistic Egypt from Alexander to Cleopatra.* New York 1985.

Rader 1981   Rader, R. 'The martyrdom of Perpetua', in *A Lost Tradition: women writers of the Early Church,* ed. P. Wilson-Kastner. Lanham, Md. 1-32.

Redfield 1978   Redfield, J. 'The women of Sparta', *Classical Journal* 73 (1978) 146-61.

Richardson 1974   Richardson, N. *The Homeric Hymn to Demeter*. Oxford.

Rist 1965   Rist, J.M. 'Hypatia', *Phoenix* 19 (1965) 214-25.

Rose   Rose, V. *Aristotelis Fragmenta*. Leipzig 1886.

Sandbach 1972   Sandbach, F.H. *Menandri Reliquiae Selectae*. Oxford.

Schanzer 1985   Schanzer, D. 'Merely a Cynic gesture'? *Rivista di Filologia* 113 (1985): 61-6.

Schaps 1977   Schaps, D. 'The woman least mentioned', *Classical Quarterly* 27: 323-30.

SEG. Supplementum Epigraphicum Graecum. 1923-.

Segal 1982   Segal, C. *Dionysiac Poetics and Euripides' Bacchae*. Princeton.

Shewring 1980   Shewring, W., tr. *The Odyssey*. Oxford 1980.

SIG Dittenberger, W. *Sylloge Inscriptionum Graecarum*, ed. 3. Leipzig 1915-24.

Simon 1978   Simon, B. *Mind and Madness in Ancient Greece: the Classical roots of modern psychiatry*. Ithaca.

Slater 1968   Slater, P. *The Glory of Hera*. Boston.

Smith 1960   Smith, W. 'The ironic structure in Alcestis', *Phoenix* 14 (1960): 127-45.

Sorum 1982   Sorum, C.E. 'The family in Sophocles' *Antigone* and *Electra*', *Classical World* 75.4 (1982): 201-11.

Stadter 1965   Stadter, P. *Plutarch's Historical Methods: an analysis of de Mulierum Virtute*. Cambridge, Mass.

Stager & Wolff 1984   Stager, L. and Wolff, S.R. 'Child sacrifice at Carthage – religious rite or population control?' *Biblical Archaeology Review* 10.1 (1984): 30-51.

Stewart 1984   Stewart, Z. 'Greek crowns and Christian martyrs', *Antiquité Paienne et Chrétienne* (Mem. A.-J. Festugière). *Cahiers d' Orientalisme* 10 (1984): 119-24.

Sulimirski 1970   Sulimirski, T. *The Sauromatians*. Ancient Peoples and Places, no. 73. New York.

Supp. Hell. Lloyd-Jones, H., and Parsons, P., edd., *Supplementum Hellenisticum*. Berlin 1983.

Thesleff 1965   Thesleff, H. *The Pythagorean Texts of the Hellenistic Period*. Abo.

Thomas 1976   Thomas, E. *Mythos und Geschichte*. Cologne.

Treggiari 1982   Treggiari, S. 'Consent to Roman marriage: some

Bibliography

    aspects of law and reality', *Classical Views* 26 (1982): 34-44.
Tyrrell 1984   Tyrrell, W.B. *Amazons: a study in Athenian mythmaking.* Baltimore.
Van Bremen 1981   Van Bremen, R. 'Women and wealth', in Cameron and Kuhrt 1981: 223-41.
Vellacott 1975   Vellacott, P. *Ironic Drama.* Cambridge.
Vidal-Naquet 1981   Vidal-Naquet, P. 'Slavery and the rule of women', in *Myth, Religion, and Society,* ed. R.L. Gordon. Cambridge.
von Bothmer 1975   von Bothmer, D. *Amazons in Greek Art.* Oxford.
W   West., M.L. *Iambi et Elegi Graeci.* Oxford 1971.
Walcot 1984   Walcot, P. 'Greek attitudes towards women: the mythological evidence', *Greece & Rome* 31 (1984): 37-47.
Warner 1976   Warner, M. *Alone of all Her Sex: the myth and cult of the Virgin Mary.* London.
Wells 1978   Wells, A.M. *Miss Marks and Miss Woolley.* Boston.
West 1978   West, M.L. *Hesiod Works and Days.* Oxford.
West 1985   West, M.L. *The Hesiodic Catalogue of Women.* Oxford.
Wicker 1975   Wicker, K.O'B. 'De Defectu Oraculorum', *Plutarch's Theological Writings and Early Christian Literature,* ed. H.D. Betz. Leiden: 131-80.
Wiedemann 1983   Wiedemann, T. 'Thucydides, women, and the limits of rational analysis', *Greece & Rome* 30 (1983) 163-70.
Wiersma 1984   Wiersma, S. 'Women in Sophocles', *Mnemosyne* 37 (1978): 25-55.
Wiesen 1976   Wiesen, D. 'The contribution of antiquity to American racial thought', *Classical Traditions in Early America,* ed. J.W. Eadie. Ann Arbor: 191-212.
Wilson 1982   Wilson, N. 'Two observations on Aristophanes' Lysistrata', *Greek, Roman and Byzantine Studies* 23 (1982): 157-63.
Winnington-Ingram 1980   Winnington-Ingram, R.P. *Sophocles: an interpretation.* Cambridge.
Winnington-Ingram 1982   Winnington-Ingram, R.P. 'Sophocles and women', *Entretiens Hardt* 29 (1982): 233-57.
Winnington-Ingram 1983   Winnington-Ingram, R.P. *Studies in Aeschylus.* Cambridge.
Wiseman 1979   Wiseman, T.P. *Clio's Cosmetics.* Leicester.

Wistrand 1976   Wistrand, E. *The So-called Laudatio Turiae.* Stud. Lat. et. Graec. Gothoburgiensia 34. Goteborg.

WLGR. Lefkowitz and Fant, 1982.

Wycherly 1978   Wycherley, R.E. *The Stones of Athens.* Princeton.

Zeitlin 1978   Zeitlin, F. 'The dynamics of misogyny in the *Oresteia', Arethusa* 11 (1978): 149-81.

Zeitlin 1982   Zeitlin, F.I. 'Cultic models of the female: rites of Dionysus and Demeter', *Arethusa* 15 (1982): 129-55.

Zintzen   Zintzen, C. *Damascii Vitae Isidori Reliquiae.* Hildesheim 1967.

Zuntz 1955   Zuntz, G. *The Political Plays of Euripides.* Manchester.

Index